Learning and Practicing Adlerian Therapy

Learning and Practicing Adlerian Therapy

Len Sperry and Vassilia Binensztok

Bassim Hamadeh, CEO and Publisher
Laura Pasquale, Specialist Acquisitions Editor
Amy Smith, Project Editor
Abbey Hastings, Associate Production Editor
Emely Villavicencio, Senior Graphic Designer
Jessica Ess, Interior Designer
Natalie Piccotti, Senior Marketing Manager
Kassie Graves, Vice President of Editorial
Jamie Giganti, Director of Academic Publishing

Printed in the United States of America.

ISBN: 978-1-5165-3694-8 (pbk) / 978-1-5165-3695-5 (br)

Brief Contents

Detailed Contents

Preface

Adlerian therapy has the distinction of being one of the first psychotherapy approaches. Over the years, many of its basic concepts and techniques have been incorporated in several other therapeutic approaches to such an extent that it has come to represent how psychotherapy is commonly practiced today. Today, the challenge for all therapy approaches is to remain relevant, which translates to being brief, accountable, and reimbursable. That means that therapists are increasingly expected to practice a brief treatment approach (five to 12 sessions) that is evidence based and achieves optimal clinical outcomes.

Many students and practicing therapists find the Adlerian approach to be most compatible with their beliefs and values and therefore want to practice it. At the same time, they are expected to practice an approach that is accountable and reimbursable. The purpose of this book is to give readers an up-to-date account of the status of the theory and practice of Adlerian therapy. It reviews both the practice of conventional Adlerian therapy and introduces a contemporary version, called Adlerian pattern-focused therapy, that can meet the needs of students and practicing therapists who want to provide a more accountable treatment approach.

Essentially, Adlerian pattern-focused therapy is neither a specific Adlerian intervention nor a set of techniques. Rather, it is a complete therapy model that embodies all basic Adlerian concepts and many techniques but incorporates a unique therapeutic strategy that significantly extends the practice of Adlerian therapy, which facilitates its accountability and reimbursability.

Learning and Practicing Adlerian Therapy highlights this approach and provides readers the experience of being "directly" involved in the therapy process. This experiential learning is facilitated with transcriptions and commentaries of therapy, from the first to the successful last session. Here is a brief overview of the book.

Chapter 1 discusses the basic concepts, premises, and theory of Adlerian psychology and its application in Adlerian therapy with individuals. Chapter 2 describes the stages and techniques of Adlerian therapy, including life style assessment, family constellation, early recollections, life style convictions, and several Adlerian interventions and techniques. The multicultural sensitivity of Adlerian therapy is also addressed. Chapter 3 introduces Adlerian pattern-focused therapy as an extension of conventional Adlerian therapy. It describes the treatment process of Adlerian pattern-focused therapy, with its emphasis on life style strategy and patterns. The ethics of Adlerian pattern-focused therapy practice and the evidence-based practice of it are also addressed. Finally, it introduces Jennifer and the 10-session therapy that is detailed in the following chapters. Chapter 4 focuses on the most important of all sessions, the first session, and what must be accomplished if client commitment and clinical success are to be achieved. Readers are invited to "sit in" on this session—and subsequent ones—through the transcription and commentary. Chapter 5 focuses on the second session and illustrates the core treatment strategy of Adlerian pattern-focused therapy in the transcription and commentary. Chapter 6 focuses on the third session and illustrates the practice of Adlerian pattern-focused therapy, including specific Adlerian and other techniques in the transcription and commentary. Chapter 7 focuses on the fourth session and continues to illustrate the therapeutic process both in session and between sessions (homework) in the transcription and commentary. Chapter 8 focuses on the process of effecting substantial client change in the middle phase of therapy: sessions 5 through 8. This is illustrated with segments of transcriptions from these sessions, with accompanying commentary. Chapter 9 focuses on the termination process in sessions 9 and 10. Consistent with Adlerian therapy, a second set of early recollections is elicited in the last session. Then, a review of progress and options for follow-up are illustrated in the transcription and commentary. Chapter 10 analyzes the criteria and markers of this successful therapy. Changes in the early recollections from the first and last sessions are interpreted, including how they reflect and "confirm" the shift from Jennifer's maladaptive to her more adaptive pattern. Finally, the future of Adlerian therapy is discussed.

It is our hope that readers will find Adlerian pattern-focused therapy—and the text's step-by-step method for learning and mastering this approach—timely and invaluable.

1

The Theory of Adlerian Therapy

Learning Objectives

In this chapter, you will learn the following:

1. Alfred Adler's personal history and professional significance
2. The key concepts of Adlerian therapy
3. The core assumptions and premises of Adlerian therapy
4. Adlerian therapy's view of personality, psychopathology, and psychotherapy
5. The strengths and limitations of this approach

There are approximately 400 approaches to psychotherapy today, and some of these will cease to exist in the coming years. Not so with Adlerian therapy, which was one of the very first psychotherapy approaches, and one that can remain viable and likely to persist for years to come. Adlerian therapy arose in the same era as Freud's psychoanalysis and Jung's analytic psychotherapy. It has influenced many current therapeutic approaches (Corey & Bitter, 2017) and has left its legacy in popular parlance with terms such as birth order, inferiority feelings, and inferiority complex. Adlerian therapy has its roots in Adlerian Psychology, which is also known as Individual Psychology.

This chapter provides an overview of the theoretical basis of Adlerian therapy. It begins with a brief biographic sketch of Alfred Adler and his enduring significance. It then defines key concepts of Adlerian psychology that are central to Adlerian therapy. Next, it discusses the core assumptions and premises. After that, it sets the stage for the rest of the book by describing the basic orientation of the approach (i.e., personality, psychopathology, and psychotherapy). Finally, it offers an evaluation of the approach regarding its strengths and limitations.

Alfred Adler: Personal History and Professional Significance

Adlerian psychology and Adlerian therapy were developed by Alfred Adler, MD (1870–1937). Adler grew up as a weak, sickly child who could not walk until four years old due to rickets. He was also tormented by his older brother. Accordingly, he admitted to feeling small, unattractive, and rejected by his mother. Nevertheless, over the course of his adolescence and early adulthood he was able to overcome his handicaps and inferiorities. He went on to complete medical studies at the University of Vienna and became an outgoing and successful physician who developed a theory of personality and psychotherapy that, in part, reflected his own early life circumstances.

Early in his professional career, Adler was invited by Freud to join the Viennese Psychoanalytic Society and remained friendly with Freud for some 10 years. He came to view Freud as inflexible in his views and obsessed with sex and death. Ultimately, Adler and Freud parted ways due to theoretical differences, and Adler developed his own approach to therapy and founded the School of Individual Psychology also known as Adlerian Psychology (Hoffman, 1994).

Subsequently, Adler influenced many others, including Karen Horney, Gordon Allport, Aaron Beck, and Abraham Maslow. Maslow, Rollo May, and Viktor Frankl all studied under Adler, and all gave him credit for having influenced their thinking. Adler paved the way for many subsequent developments in psychotherapy including humanistic psychology, cognitive therapy, cognitive behavior therapy, and the constructivist therapies. Adler's approach was implemented in several modalities including group therapy, child guidance, family therapy, and couples therapy. In North America, Rudolf Dreikurs, MD, and several others implemented and extended Adler's approach in these various modalities (Dreikurs, 1967).

FIGURE 1.1. Alfred Adler, MD, founder of individual psychology

Key Concepts of Adlerian Psychology

Adler considered all behavior as purposive and interactive. Both individuals and social systems were viewed as holistic, and individuals were motived to seek "belonging" or significance and meaning in their lives by the way they functioned in social systems. He contended that it was within the family constellation that individuals first learn how to belong and interact, and the family was reflective of the child's first experience of both culture and the larger society. Adler emphasized the unique and private beliefs and strategies of individuals (i.e., "private logic," that individuals create in childhood and which serve as a reference for attitudes, private views of self, others, and the world, and behavior which he called the "lifestyle" and "lifestyle convictions").

Individuals form their lifestyle as they endeavor to relate to others, to overcome "feelings of inferiority," and to find a sense of belonging. Furthermore, Adler believed that healthy and productive individuals are characterized by a community feeling and its action line, "social interest" (i.e., concern for the needs of others and the community, whereas those with poor adjustment or psychopathology show little social interest and tend to be self-focused) (Ansbacher, 1992; Ansbacher & Ansbacher, 1956).

Adler contended that there is a unity to an individual's personality and that each individual fashions that unity. As such, the individual can be considered both the artist and the portrait. Accordingly, when individuals can change their concept of self, they can change the portrait that they paint with their lives. The theory of Adlerian psychology is nicely captured in the following seven basic concepts (Bitter, 2007; Carlson, Watts, & Maniacci, 2006; Mosak & Maniacci, 1999).

Birth Order

Birth order refers to the order in which a child is born in their family. Adler argued that birth order influences personality development and lifestyle. Birth order is characterized as ordinal position (i.e., actual order of birth of siblings) and psychological position, the role the child assumes in interactions with other siblings. Five psychological birth-order positions have been described: oldest born, second born, only children, middle children, and youngest born (Carlson & Englar-Carlson, 2017). While it is possible to make some generalizations about birth order (e.g., that younger and only children tend to be pampered and spoiled), it is ultimately the individual who determines how he or she views his or her position in the family.

Early Recollections

Early recollections are recalled stories of single, specific incidents from childhood. Neurologically they are called episodic or autobiographical memories. Psychologically, they are considered a projective technique (Mosak & Di Pietro, 2006; Clark, 2002). In Adlerian therapy, they are understood dynamically, meaning that the act of recollecting and remembering them is a present activity, while their historical validity is not relevant. Instead, they mirror presently held attitudes, convictions, evaluations, and biases.

Family Constellation

Family constellation refers to the early developmental influences on an individual. It represents how an individual's family of origin functioned in childhood. It reflects the nature of relationships among parents, siblings, and sometimes extended family, family culture, and key individuals from the neighborhood or community. It describes these family dynamics and includes birth order, expectations, family values, and how problems and conflicts were handled. Family constellation strongly influences lifestyle.

Inferiority Complex

Adler observed that a child experiences feelings of inferiority as the result of being around stronger and more capable adults. As he or she grows, the child becomes obsessed by these feelings of inferiority and compensates by striving for power and recognition. If he or she has failed to meet certain life tasks by "compensation" (developing extra strength in other parts), or through "overcompensation" (converting the weakness into a strength), he or she will develop an inferiority complex.

Lifestyle

Lifestyle refers to the pattern of an individual's striving toward significance and belonging: It is one's movement through time and changing situations (challenges) and the process adopted for coping (Rasmussen, 2010). This pattern manifests early in life and can be observed as a theme throughout a lifetime. It permeates all aspects of perception and action (Sperry & Sperry, 2012). It includes an individual's attitudes and convictions about how to find one's place in the world and instructions for how to belong. By understanding another's lifestyle, one can make sense of that individual's behavior.

Private Logic

Private logic, also called private sense, is the reasoning invented by an individual to justify a self-serving behavior or lifestyle. It contrasts with common logic or common sense, which represents society's cumulative, consensual reasoning. Another way of thinking about private logic is that it involves "ideas conceived in childhood that comprise one's deeply established personal beliefs or constructs" (Carlson & Englar-Carlson, 2017, p. 142).

Social Interest

Also called Gemeinschaftsgefühl and community feeling, social interest is a central tenet of this approach. Social interest is "(a)n interest in the interest of others, behaviors and attitudes that display a sense of fellow feeling, responsibility and community with others, not just for today but for generations to come" (Carlson, Watts, & Maniacci, 2006, p. 278). If the feeling of inferiority is not too great, an individual will strive to be worthwhile and on the useful side of life. In contrast, individuals experience maladjustment or psychological disorder as inferiority feelings, underdeveloped social interest, and an exaggerated goal of personal superiority increase. Such individuals may develop symptoms when they try to solve problems in a self-centered "private sense" rather than a task-centered "common sense." Table 1.1 summarizes these seven key concepts.

Core Assumptions

The core assumptions or premises of a therapeutic approach form the foundation on which basic theory, conceptualization, and therapeutic interventions are based. Here is a brief review of six basic assumptions underlying Adlerian therapy (Mosak, & Maniacci, 1999).

Holism

Adler believed that an individual is best understood as a whole, self-conscious being that functions as a totality, rather than as a collection of drives and instincts. The assumption of holism enables one to understand the individual as a totality. It is noteworthy that the term "individual psychology" does not refer to the word "individual," but rather refers to indivisibility, which denotes being that is whole and undivided. Accordingly, Adlerian therapists focus on what the individual is doing instead of focusing on various parts of the individual. This theoretical distinction of focusing on the individual as a whole and integrated being assumes the element of responsibility. Thus, instead of viewing ambivalence as a conflict among various parts of the individual's personality, Adlerian therapists conceptualize ambivalence as the result of an individual's conflicting goals and choices.

TABLE 1.1 Some Key Concepts

Birth order: An individual's position within the family of origin. It reflects both biological and psychological position (i.e., first born, middle child, youngest child).

Early recollections: A projective technique used to determine a client's self-view, view of others, world view, and his or her overall strategy in dealing with others and life's challenges.

Family constellation: A description of family dynamics including one's relationships with other family members, birth order, expectations, family values, and how conflict is handled.

Inferiority complex: Feeling that one is not as good as others, which drives the individual to overcompensate, resulting in either extreme achievement or asocial behavior.

Lifestyle: The pattern of an individual's striving toward significance and belonging; manifests early in life and a consistent theme thereafter.

Private logic: Private reasoning that justifies self-serving behavior and beliefs. Also called private sense, the opposite of common sense.

Social interest: An individual's sense of connection to community and willingness to contribute to the well-being of others.

Teleology

In addition, Adler believed that behavior, be it thoughts, feelings, or actions, is best understood as goal directed or teleological. That means that behavior is purposive and in line with the individual's lifestyle goals and movement, even if the individual is not consciously aware of the purpose. Teleology also addresses the purpose of conflict. Adler believed that individuals think, feel, and react for a reason. He developed his theory at a time when other theories focused on explaining personality development and pathology as rooted in the individual's childhood. While acknowledging that the past plays a critical role in creating the foundation of personality, Adler insisted that current behavior is influenced by one's past but is also influenced by one's goals for the future. This conceptualization is called fictional finalism. He observed that individuals live by fictional ideals that have no relation to reality and cannot be empirically tested and confirmed. Adler's conclusion was that individuals are motivated more by what they expect of the future than of the past. Thus, if an individual believes that heaven is reserved for those who are good and hell for those who are bad, this ideal will likely affect how that individual lives (Mitchell, 2011).

Phenomenology

Phenomenology is the branch of philosophy that focuses on consciousness and direct experiences. It means that individuals view and experience things from their own unique perspectives. Therefore, Adlerian therapists are not as concerned with facts as they are with an individual's perceptions of the facts. The goal is to view reality the way the client views it. Instead of focusing on a universal truth, Adlerian therapists are more interested on the unique ways individuals make meaning. That means seeking to understand an individual's personal philosophy and what truth is for that unique individual.

Soft Determinism

Adlerian therapy is based on soft determinism. This differed markedly from other early approaches that were based on hard determinism. Hard determinism is a view of life and a philosophical and scientific perspective that assumes that environment, heredity, unconscious impulses, defense mechanisms, and other influences determine the reason individuals act the way they do. From this perspective, individuals are not responsible for their actions because they do not possess freedom to choose.

In contrast, soft determinism holds that individuals can make choices and so are responsible for their actions. While soft determinism underlies many current therapeutic approaches, Adler developed his theory and approach at a time when psychoanalysis and behaviorism espoused hard determinism (Ansbacher & Ansbacher, 1956). Instead, Adler insisted that individuals author the script of their lives and asserted the notion of the "creative self," which means that an individual "creates" his or her personality and is responsible for his or her actions (Mosak, & Maniacci, 1999). Accordingly, the individual cannot blame others or uncontrollable forces for his or her current condition. Furthermore, freedom of choice is central in the practice of Adlerian therapy, with its focus on empowerment and encouragement with clients.

Social Embeddedness

Adler insisted that individuals are social beings and require the support of a community. They do not develop in isolation. Instead, they find a place of significance or belonging in a social context. Accordingly, an individual's behavior is best understood in relation to culture and society. The family, of course, is the first experience for most individuals of social embeddedness, and even if it is not immediately apparent to many individuals in the dominant culture, there are many aspects related to ethnicity, culture, and gender that are passed on in the DNA of individuals and reinforced in family life. This is especially significant in people from marginalized cultures or religions, people who are gay, lesbian, fluid, or trans, and other people who experience discrimination.

Health and Pathology

Adlerian therapy views the healthy individual as one who engages in life experiences with confidence and optimism. There is a sense of belonging and contributing and the serene knowledge that one can be acceptable to others although imperfect (Sperry, 2008). Subjectivity is central for understanding the client, specifically the individual's cognitions and beliefs about self, others, and the world. Though it shares much with psychodynamic approaches, Adler's theory focuses on consciousness rather than unconsciousness, because he was convinced that the most important life problems are social and relational and thus the individual must be considered within the social context (Sperry, 2008). The theory proposes that an individual's basic motivation is to find a sense of belonging and connectedness with others. Furthermore, lifestyle convictions are influenced by one's family constellation (i.e., birth order, sibling and parental relationships, and family values) (Sperry, 2008).

Once the person has adopted a "mistaken goal," he or she will formulate other misconceptions to support the "faulty logic." Accordingly, the goal of psychotherapy for this approach is to correct mistakes in perception and logic (i.e., faulty lifestyle convictions) that individuals formed in their effort to relate to others and to overcome feelings of inferiority.

Individuals develop four lifestyle convictions: a self-view—the convictions one has about who they are; a self-ideal—the convictions of what they should be or are obliged to be to have a place; a world view—their picture of the world or convictions about the way life is and what the world demands of them; and their ethical convictions—a personal moral code (Mosak, & Maniacci, 1999). When there is conflict between the self-concept and the ideal, inferiority feelings develop. It is important to note that feelings of inferiority are not considered abnormal. However, when the individual begins to act inferior rather than feel inferior, the individual expresses an "inferiority complex." Thus, while inferiority feelings are universal and normal, the inferiority complex reflects the discouragement of a limited segment of our society and is usually abnormal (Sperry & Sperry, 2018).

Individuals strive to attain goals that provide them with a place in their world, which provides them security and enhanced self-esteem. If they strive solely for their own personal gain, Adler considered such individuals socially useless and possibly pathological. On the other hand, if the purpose of an individual's strivings is to overcome life's problems, the individual is engaged in the striving for self-realization and making the world a better place to live. This is a marker or indicator of psychological health.

Adler proposed a useful typology of psychological health and psychopathology (Mosak, & Maniacci, 1999). He contended that good adjustment or psychological health is striving on the "commonly useful side" while poor adjustment and psychopathology is striving on the "commonly useless side." Furthermore, Adler believed that psychopathology represented disturbances or dysfunction not only in the individual, but in the social situation as well. Adler presumes individuals possess the innate potential for social interest. Not to want to help one's neighbor is one of the characteristics of maladjustment (Sperry, 2008). The individual whose social interest is well developed finds the solution to problems, feels at home in the world, and views life's circumstances more clearly, whereas individuals with poor adjustment and psychopathology have little or no social interest and are not interested in others. Personality disorders are presumed to stem from faulty lifestyle convictions or early maladaptive schemas (Sperry, 2015).

Basic Orientation of Adlerian Therapy

Most therapeutic approaches elaborate their basic orientation. Typically, this includes three basic considerations: (a) how personality develops; (b) how this process becomes disordered; and (c) how this distorted process can be reversed. In short, these reflect personality development, psychopathology, and psychotherapy. Here is how Adlerian Therapy addresses each of these three considerations. This characterization provides a useful summary of the theory underlying this approach (Sperry, 2010).

Personality Development

The basic human motivation is to belong, and individuals develop within a family context called the family constellation. In this context, individuals create their own subjective interpretation of life events based on their unique private logic, which becomes their lifestyle or cognitive map. This map subsequently guides their perceptions and actions. It contains subjective convictions about self-view, world view, and conclusions and life strategies that reflect the life narrative. Healthy functioning is an outcome of social interest (i.e., concern for others).

Psychopathology

Psychopathology reflects the way an individual "arranges" symptoms that serve as excuses for failing to meet the tasks of life or responsibilities, as well as for safeguarding self-esteem. Psychopathology reflects individuals' self-interest and discouragement and is manifested in their faulty lifestyle convictions (i.e., core convictions that run counter to social interest). These are also called maladaptive schemas and are summarized as their "basic mistakes."

Psychotherapy

Psychotherapy is a change process with the primary goal of increasing social interest. This can be accomplished in several ways, ranging from modifying basic mistakes and behavior to replacing maladaptive thoughts and behaviors with more life-giving ones. Typically, the process has four stages or phases: establishing and maintaining an effective therapeutic relationship, assessment or lifestyle investigation, insight and constructive action, and reorientation. These processes tend to be continuous and iterative throughout the course of treatment. Table 1.2 summarizes the basic orientation.

Adlerian Therapy: Strengths and Limitations

Strengths

In many respects, Adlerian therapy is the intellectual source or taproot from which many current psychotherapeutic systems have emerged. These include rational emotive behavior therapy, cognitive therapy, cognitive behavioral therapy (CBT), existential therapy, logotherapy, solution-focused therapy, and the constructivist therapy approaches. In some ways, object relations therapy and self-psychology owe much to Adlerian concepts and methods. Adlerian therapy is applicable to many, if not most, clinical presentations and can be practiced in both brief and long-term treatment contexts, and in various intervention modalities with individuals, couples, families, and groups (Sperry, 2008).

TABLE 1.2 Basic Orientation

Personality Development	Basic motivation is *to belong* and develops within a *family constellation* wherein individuals create their own subjective interpretation of life events based on their unique *private logic* which becomes their *lifestyle*, which subsequently guides their perceptions and actions and contains subjective convictions about *self-view, world-view, and conclusions or life strategies*. Healthy functioning is an outcome of *social interest* (i.e., concern for other).
Psychopathology	Reflects the manner in which an individual *"arranges" symptoms* that serve as excuses for failing to meet *life tasks* and safeguard self-esteem. Reflects self-interest and *discouragement* and faulty lifestyle convictions and *"basic mistakes."*
Psychotherapy	Involves four stages: establishing and maintaining an effective therapeutic relationship; lifestyle investigation; insight and constructive action; and reorientation. Continuous throughout the course of treatment; primary goal is to increase *social interest*.

Limitations

However, while Adler's approach has influenced, directly or indirectly, most current therapy approaches, relatively few students and therapists are aware of this fact. In contrast, CBT is the most widely used approach in North America and many parts of the world at large. This is largely because of CBT's many training programs and the extensive amount of empirical research, which demonstrated efficacy and effectiveness. Furthermore, in this era of accountability, because CBT has been designated as an evidence-based approach, CBT-oriented therapists are more easily reimbursed for therapeutic services (Sperry, 2018). Adlerian therapy, by comparison, has relatively fewer training programs and less research supporting its efficacy and effectiveness, which are requisites for achieving evidence-based status.

Concluding Note

Alfred Adler pioneered a holistic theory of personality, psychotherapy, and psychopathology. This chapter has described the theoretical basis for Adlerian therapy, including its basic concepts and core assumptions as well as its strengths and limitations. Chapter 2 will describe and illustrate the actual practice of Adlerian therapy. It emphasizes the treatment process and various therapeutic interventions.

References

Ansbacher, H. L. (1992). Alfred Adler's concepts of community feeling and of social interest and the relevance of community feeling for old age. *Individual Psychology, 48*(4), 402–412.

Ansbacher, H. L., & Ansbacher, R. R. (Eds.). (1956). *The individual psychology of Alfred Adler.* New York, NY: Harper & Row.

Bitter, J. R. (2007.). Am I an Adlerian? *Journal of Individual Psychology, 63*(1), 3–31.

Carlson, J., & Englar-Carlson, M. (2017). *Adlerian psychotherapy.* Washington DC: American Psychological Association.

Carlson, J., Watts, R. E., & Maniacci, M. (2006). *Adlerian therapy: Theory and process.* Washington DC: American Psychological Association.

Clark, A. J. (2002). Early recollections: Theory and practice in counseling and psychotherapy. New York, NY: Brunner-Routledge.

Corey, G., & Bitter, J. R. (2017). Adlerian therapy. In G. Corey (Ed.), *Theory and practice of counseling and psychotherapy* (10th ed.) (pp. 95–128). Boston, MA: Cengage.

Dreikurs, R. (1967). *Psychodynamics, psychotherapy, and counseling: The collected papers of Rudolf Dreikurs, M.D.* Chicago, IL: The Alfred Adler Institute.

Hoffman, E. (1994). *The drive for self: Alfred Adler and the founding of Individual Psychology.* Reading, MA: Addison-Wesley.

Mitchell, G. (2011). *Alfred Adler and Adlerian individual psychology.* Retrieved from https://mind-development.eu/adler.html

Mosak, H., & Di Pietro, R. (2006). *Early recollections: Interpretative method and application.* New York, NY: Routledge.

Mosak, H. H., & Maniacci, M. (1999). *A primer of Adlerian psychology.* New York, NY: Brunner-Routledge.

Rasmussen, P. R. (2010). *The quest to feel good.* New York, NY: Routledge.

Sperry, L. (2008). Adlerian psychotherapy. In K. Jordan (Ed.). *The quick theory reference guide: A resource for expert and novice mental health professionals* (pp. 23–29). New York, NY: Nova Science Publishers.

Sperry, L. (2010). *Highly effective therapy: Developing essential clinical competencies in counseling and psychotherapy.* New York, NY: Routledge.

Sperry, L. (2015). Personality disorders. In L. Sperry, J. Carlson, J. Duba-Sauerheber, & J. Sperry (Eds.). *Psychopathology and psychotherapy: DSM-5 diagnosis, case conceptualization and treatment,* (3rd ed.) (pp. 27–61). New York, NY: Routledge.

Sperry, L. (2018). Achieving evidence-based status for Adlerian therapy: Why it is needed and how to accomplish it. *Journal of Individual Psychology, 74*(3), 247–264.

Sperry, L., & Sperry, J. (2012). *Case conceptualization: Mastering this competency with ease and confidence.* New York, NY: Routledge

Sperry, J. & Sperry, L. (2018). Individual psychology (Adler). In V. Zeigler-Hill & T. K. Shackelford (Eds.), *Encyclopedia of personality and individual differences* (pp. 1–4). New York, NY: Springer.

2

The Practice of Adlerian Therapy

Learning Objectives

In this chapter, you will learn the following:

1. The varieties of Adlerian therapy: individual, group, family, and couples therapy
2. The process of change in Adlerian therapy
3. The treatment process and the therapeutic relationship
4. Assessment, including elicitation of family constellation and early recollections
5. Treatment goals, case conceptualization, interventions, and evaluation of therapy
6. The multicultural sensitivity of Adlerian therapy
7. A case example of how Adlerian therapy is practiced

Individuals typically seek therapy to better understand their life circumstances and to make changes in their behaviors. The process of change in Adlerian therapy addresses both understanding and behavior change. Typically, it involves an assessment of individuals' birth order, early recollections, social context, and other external dynamics, including parental influences. The purpose of this assessment is to understand how these various factors have influenced self-worth, expectations, and behavior, so that individuals can better understand and accept themselves relative to both early childhood and current experiences and to encourage positive change in both beliefs and behavior.

This chapter begins with an overview of Adlerian therapy practice. It then identifies the varieties of Adlerian therapy. Next, it moves to the treatment process of this approach and starts with a discussion of the Adlerian view of the change process and the therapeutic relationship. This is followed by a discussion of both assessment and treatment strategies. Assessment strategies include a detailed inquiry and the elicitation of family constellation and early recollection material. This is followed by a discussion of Adlerian case conceptualization, treatment goals, interventions, and treatment evaluation. An extended case example illustrates how Adlerian therapy is commonly practiced today.

Overview of Adlerian Therapy

An Adlerian therapist assists clients in understanding their thoughts, drives, and emotions that influence their lifestyles. Clients are also encouraged to acquire a more positive and productive way of life by developing new insights, skills, and behaviors (Carlson, Watts, & Maniacci, 2006). However, the basic or "strategic goal of Adlerian psychotherapy is to foster the client's sense of community feeling" (Carlson, Watts, & Maniacci, 2006, p. 134). These goals are achieved through the four phases of Adlerian therapy:

1. Engagement wherein a trusting therapeutic relationship is developed between the therapist and the client and they agree to work together to effectively address the presenting problem or concern
2. Assessment in which the therapist elicits the client's personal history, family history, early recollections, beliefs, feelings, pattern, motivation, and readiness for treatment
3. Awareness and insight in which clients are helped to develop new ways of thinking about life and the presenting problem or concern
4. Reorientation wherein therapists encourage clients to engage in more effective behavior that reinforce this new insight or further facilitates it

Varieties of Adlerian Therapy

There are several varieties of Adlerian therapy. They include long-term individual therapy, brief individual therapy, play therapy, group therapy, couples therapy, and family therapy. Common to these various types is a process that guides individuals to release their unproductive values, beliefs, feelings, and behavior and to refocus on more productive ones that foster social interest. The overall goal of this type of therapy is to change destructive self-directed beliefs and behaviors and equip clients with the necessary tools that will allow them to become confident and socially empowered (Sperry, 2008). The remainder of this book focuses on a brief form of Adlerian therapy with individuals.

Change Process in Adlerian Therapy

Adlerian therapy is optimistic in its emphasis on clients' potential for growth and change. Because it is grounded in a growth model rather than a pathology model, clients are viewed as being discouraged rather than disordered. That translates to mean that clients need new skills and a new perspective on living. Accordingly, Adlerian therapy is more about encouraging and educating clients rather than curing them (Carlson & Carlson-Englar, 2017). Besides this general understanding of the change process, this approach views the change process as specific and subjective. This means that "Adlerian therapists realize that all clients enter into treatment with different levels of readiness.... The state of change represents when people change, and the Adlerian therapist identifies the stage and tailors their treatment process (how people change) to match the stage" (Carlson & Carlson-Englar, 2017, pp. 53–54).

Awareness is another aspect of the change process. While clients are not always fully aware of their specific patterns and goals, through analysis of birth order, early recollections, and coping style, the therapist helps clients recognize their pattern of limiting and problematic beliefs and behaviors. This allows clients to view life from another perspective, so they can explore and practice new behaviors and a new orientation to life.

Treatment Process of Adlerian Therapy

The therapeutic process in Adlerian therapy consists of five factors: therapeutic relationship, lifestyle assessment, case conceptualization and intervention planning, intervention implementation, and evaluation and termination. The immediate goal is resolution of the presenting problem, while the primary goal of treatment is to increase social interest (Ansbacher & Ansbacher, 1956). Table 2.1 summarizes these factors.

TABLE 2.1 Process of Adlerian therapy

Therapeutic relationship

The relationship is characterized by mutual respect and equality. Client and therapist are considered collaborative partners wherein clients are expected to assume an active role in the change process.

Assessment

Assessment focuses on both the current situation and predisposing factors (i.e., lifestyle analysis). This analysis includes elicitation of family constellation and early developmental experiences, including early recollections, to derive the individual's lifestyle convictions.

Case conceptualization

Lifestyle information is summarized into a conceptualization, which is collaboratively discussed and modified with the client. The conceptualization helps clients understand who and how they become who they are and increases their awareness of their faulty logic and patterns.

Intervention

The focus of treatment is faulty lifestyle convictions and basic mistakes. The basic goals are to increase social interest and modify faulty lifestyle convictions, while the basic therapeutic strategies are cognitive restructuring and fostering insight and constructive action. Interventions include lifestyle assessment, interpretation, encouragement, and acting "as if."

Intervention evaluation

Usually, a second set of early recollections (ERs) are elicited as termination nears. These are compared to the themes in the first set that are elicited at the outset of treatment to assess change.

Therapeutic Relationship

Adlerian therapy fosters a therapeutic relationship, also known as the therapeutic alliance, that is a collaborative alliance among equal individuals. That means that the therapist attempts to establish and maintain a relationship that is characterized as cooperative, empathic, and non-dogmatic. More specifically, the Adlerian therapist does not assume the role of expert who interprets and advises the client, but rather joins the client as a fellow traveler in life's journey. Instead, therapists serve as role models of psychological health and social interest for their clients. Through respectful dialogue and encouragement, clients can correct mistaken convictions, attitudes, and feelings about themselves and the world, as well as change their behavior (Carlson, Watts & Maniacci, 2006).

Assessment

The basic Adlerian constructs to be assessed include family constellation and early recollections. Inferences are drawn from this data and then formulated into an Adlerian case conceptualization. Besides eliciting traditional intake material (e.g., present concerns, mental status exam, and general social, occupational, and developmental history), the therapist collects and analyzes the client's family constellation and lifestyle convictions (Sperry & Sperry, 2012). This information is most useful in specifying a case conceptualization, particularly the clinical formulation part, which is an explanation of why and how the client perceives, feels, and acts in a patterned and predictable fashion (Mosak & Maniacci, 1999; Sperry 2015).

Family Constellation

The family constellation is comprised of information about the client's relationships with family members, as well as the relationships between other family members. It consists of the client's birth order; identifications with parents, siblings, and peers; family values; family narrative; and the way the client found a sense of belonging in his or her family. Both biological and psychological birth order should be taken into account, as well as family values and the client's sense of belonging within the family. The client is asked to describe what it was like growing up in the home and relationships with parents and siblings. Parental relationships and the way in which family members dealt with conflicts, and the way parents disciplined children, should also be explored (Carlson & Carlson-Englar, 2017).

Family Constellation Assessment

Table 2.2 gives questions that are useful in eliciting the family constellation.

Early Recollections

Early recollections are used as a projective assessment to elicit a client's self-view, world view, and view of others. Because a client's recollection of his or her earliest memories reflects past childhood events in light of current lifestyle convictions, early recollections are a powerful projective technique that quickly and accurately access a client's self-other schemas (i.e., the way clients view themselves, others, and the world) (Sperry & Sperry, 2012). Early recollections also help reveal a client's level of social interest (Carlson & Carlson-Englar, 2017).

The therapist elicits three or more memories, and the description of these memories are analyzed according to themes and developmental maturity and from these derives the client's lifestyle convictions, which reflect the impact of the client's family constellation. Typically, these recollections should occur before the age of eight. Each recollection should be a memory that

TABLE 2.2 Eliciting Family Constellation Data

What was it like growing up in your home?
What was it like being the oldest (youngest, middle, or only) child in your family?
Please describe your relationships with your parents. Which one were you most like?
Who was your mother's favorite among your siblings? Your father's favorite?
Please describe the relationship between your parents. Who made the big decisions?
How did they solve problems? How did they deal with conflicts? Did they show affection openly? Who was the breadwinner? Who was the disciplinarian?
Who did you go to when you were hurt or frightened?
What were the family values? What were you expected to be or do when you grew up?
Please describe your relationships with your siblings.
Who got the best grades? Who was the most athletic? Had the most friends?
Who got into trouble the most? How are they doing now?

the client specifically recalls, rather than one that someone else mentioned to the client. Also, the experience should involve a single event and the therapist should record the client's age at the time, what happened, who was involved, and what each individual was doing and saying during the event. Finally, the most vivid part of the memory, and the client's associated thoughts and feelings, should be elicited (Mosak & Di Pietro, 2006).

Early Recollections Assessment

Table 2.3 provides a method for eliciting early recollections.

Lifestyle Convictions

Lifestyle convictions are conclusions about a client's inner world that are derived from information about family constellation, birth order, early recollections, and overcompensation. They also represent the client's basic pattern (Sperry, 2015).

Here is a formula statement that summarizes these convictions into a life strategy or pattern:

- I am.... (self-view)
- Life is.... People are.... (world-view)
- Therefore.... (life strategy)

TABLE 2.3 Eliciting Early Recollections

Say: "Think back before to your early life—the age of eight—and tell me your first memory. It should be about a single experience that you specifically recall, rather than one that someone told you happened. Not a repeated experience but a single one."
If the client has difficulty identifying a memory, prompt him or her by asking about a memorable birthday, the first day of school, a specific vacation, etc.
For each memory, ask how old the client was at the time; next, elicit the sequence of the memory. Ask how it began, who else was involved, what each person was doing or saying, and how it ended. Then, elicit the most vivid moment in the sequence, what the client felt at that moment, and what the client was thinking at that moment.

Case Conceptualization

"Case conceptualization is a method and clinical strategy for obtaining and organizing information about a client, understanding and explaining the client's situation and maladaptive patterns, guiding and focusing treatment, anticipating challenges and roadblocks, and preparing for successful termination" (Sperry & Sperry, 2012, p. 4). Like other theory-based case conceptualization methods, the Adlerian case conceptualization method includes clinical, cultural, and treatment formulations that emphasize the client's unique lifestyle and lifestyle conviction. The clinical formulation part of an Adlerian case conceptualization helps clients understand who they are and how they become who they are. It also helps clients to increase awareness of their faulty logic and lifestyle convictions. It provides therapists with an understanding of lifestyle dynamics relevant to treatment planning. The cultural formulation part provides an explanation, in terms of cultural dynamics, in relation to the client's lifestyle dynamics. The treatment formulation part of the case conceptualization includes a plan to modify faulty lifestyle convictions and basic mistakes and to increase social interest. Information from these four components is summarized into a case conceptualization, which is collaboratively discussed with the client.

While most case conceptualization models share several common elements, there are at least three signature elements of Adlerian case conceptualization that make it different from other case conceptualization models. These elements are predisposition, treatment goals, and treatment interventions. It is not surprising that predisposition in the Adlerian therapy approach emphasizes family constellation and lifestyle convictions. Similarly, the unique treatment goals involve increasing social interest and constructive action. Likewise, the unique or signature treatment interventions in this approach include lifestyle assessment, early recollection analysis, encouragement, the push button technique, and acting "as if" (Sperry & Sperry, 2012).

Treatment Goals

Once the initial assessment and case conceptualization has been completed, the goals for treatment can be set. The goal of treatment is more than symptom relief or problem resolution. Rather, it is a new orientation to life and a way of making a difference in the community. To the extent that therapy is successful, the client will experience more social interest. This approach assumes that the values a client holds and lives by are learned, and when they no longer work and lead to suffering or unhappiness, the client can relearn values and fashion a lifestyle that works more effectively (Sperry, 2008).

The client's lifestyle convictions can also be understood as schemas and self-other schemas (self-view and world view). Because such maladaptive schemas or basic mistakes are believed to be true for the individual, the individual acts accordingly. Adler noted that these basic mistakes are overgeneralizations, such as "people are hostile," "life is dangerous," and "life doesn't give me any breaks." These overgeneralizations are expressed in the client's physical behavior, language, values, and dreams (Sperry & Sperry, 2012). Accordingly, the goal of treatment is re-education and reorientation of the client to schemas that work "better" (Carlson & Carlson-Englar, 2017).

Furthermore, Adlerian therapists tend to be action orientated. That means that many believe that insight is necessary but not sufficient. For change to occur, behavior must change. Insight reflects the client's understanding of the purposeful nature of behavior, but it must be followed by action. In other words, insight is understanding translated into action.

Interventions

A main attraction of Adlerian therapy for therapists and students is its flexibility and eclectic approach to planning and implementing treatment. This means that a therapist who utilizes the Adlerian philosophy and lifestyle assessments, has the flexibility to choose specific interventions and techniques from various other therapeutic approaches as well as those that are unique to Adlerian therapy.

Many Adlerian therapy interventions and techniques are action oriented. They facilitate lifestyle and behavior changes while working to help the individual learn to counteract discouragement, enhance self-efficacy, and increase self-esteem (Sperry, 2008). Change can be effected by employing therapeutic tactics such as humor, frequent use of encouragement and support, and the use of language that avoids moralizing. Some Adlerian therapy techniques and tactics are activity focused. They include creative and dramatic approaches to treatment such as task setting, acting "as if," and the push button technique (Mosak & Maniacci, 1998). (Chapter 3 provides descriptions and examples of these techniques.) In addition to providing clients the opportunity to rehearse new life skills, the use of such techniques allows clients to make choices about the roles and behavior patterns they would do better to discard and those to keep.

Intervention Evaluation

Typically, Adlerian therapists evaluate therapeutic outcome by eliciting a second set of early recollections. Early recollections, collected at the outset of therapy, are called pre-intervention ERs, while those collected near the end of therapy are referred to as post-intervention ERs. "Changes in ERs frequently occur in therapy and these changes appear to be in accord with clients' changed perception of life" (Mosak & DiPietro, 2006, p. 203). We would add, that pre- to post-intervention changes also include changes in life strategy (i.e., from a maladaptive pattern to a more adaptive pattern). Our experience has been that in focusing on shifting the maladaptive pattern to a more adaptive one, the client's self-other schemas (self-view and world view) also shift in a healthier direction, even though the therapeutic focus is on the life strategy and not self-other schemas.

Multicultural Sensitivity of Adlerian Therapy

So, how sensitive is Adlerian therapy to multicultural concerns? The answer is very sensitive. For example, "[m]any of the core aspects of Adlerian psychotherapy mirror recommendations for effective multicultural psychotherapy. These include the importance of an egalitarian, respectful, and cooperative counselor-client relationship (therapeutic alliance); the focus on social equality and social justice; taking a holistic approach that considers mind, body, and spirit; the need to view people contextually, in their family, social and cultural contexts; and the emphasis on strengths, optimism, encouragement, empowerment, advocacy, and support" (Carlson, & Englar-Carlson, 2017, pp. 106–107).

Furthermore, "the characteristics and assumptions of Adlerian psychology are congruent with the cultural values of many racial-ethnic, minority groups and ... the Adlerian therapeutic process is respectful of cultural diversity" (Carlson, Watts, & Maniacci, 2006, p. 32). It has also been observed that the "individual's unique subjective interpretation and perception are part of Adlerian theory, and the client's culture, values and views are honored and accepted. Adlerian [therapy] goals are not aimed at deciding for clients what they should change about themselves. Rather, the practitioner works in collaboration with clients and their family networks" (Arcineiga & Newlon, 2003, p. 436).

Adlerian Therapy—Case Example

Jeffrey is a 39-year-old married Caucasian male who is the vice president of sales for an international software corporation. He was referred for therapy by the HR director of his firm because of increasing depression, difficulty concentrating, and insomnia. It appears his symptoms began soon after his wife, Jane, was diagnosed with breast cancer. Jeffrey was devastated by her diagnosis, presumably because of his reliance on her for emotional support. Since she started chemotherapy treatments, Jeffery began calling his mother regularly in disbelief that Jane was sick.

He is the youngest of three siblings in a family that valued financial success and public recognition. As a young child, Jeffrey experienced severe allergic reactions, which led to several emergency room visits with his mother at his side. She was described as caring, supportive, and conflict avoidant, while his father was described as hardworking, emotionally absent, and demanding. Jeffrey became successful and self-absorbed like his father.

Jeffrey described himself as a "party animal" in college but graduated with a degree in management. Afterwards, he rose quickly to become the top sales executive at his firm. He is an avid basketball fan and a competitive bridge player. He met Jane through social friends and describes her as supportive and caring.

The following lifestyle analysis was developed based on data gleaned from family constellation and early recollections. The following core convictions of his lifestyle became the focus of Adlerian therapy:

SELF-VIEW: Views himself as strong, superior, and entitled

WORLD-VIEW: Views life as a banquet table for him to enjoy at any time, with others in his service

LIFE STRATEGY: His basic strategies for dealing with problems and resolving conflicts is to act upset, make demands, and expect to be taken care of and rewarded

Jeffrey's basic mistakes include his belief that he is the center of his universe, that life should be enjoyable, and that others are there to meet his needs. He relies on the women in his life to support him and believes that men are superior to women and that they should never challenge nor make demands on him.

Therapy began by addressing his depressive symptoms and processing his mistaken beliefs. Jeffrey was quite intrigued that acting upset and demanding were his life strategy and were his ways of compensating for his health problems as a child. With time, Jeffrey came to realize that while these worked for his father and him earlier in his life, they were less effective now, particularly since Jane's medical condition worsened. It had never occurred to him that negotiation and conflict resolution were the responsibility of both spouses. For much of his life, he had simply modeled his father's non-negotiating and demanding strategies. In time, he was able to develop healthier ones.

As he became more proficient in these alternative strategies, Jeffrey was more receptive to therapeutically processing his sense of superiority and entitlement. As termination neared, his depression had resolved and his self-view and world-view had moderated. Furthermore, he became more accepting of Jane's medical condition and the necessity of supporting and caring for her.

Concluding Note

Adlerian therapy is a vigorously optimistic and inspiring approach to therapy. Problems or dysfunction results from discouragement and a lack of social interest. The treatment process stresses education to promote growth and change in lifestyle convictions. Therapy with clients focuses on increasing social interest, encouraging responsibility for behavior, and supporting behavioral change. Insight is used therapeutically as a tool to facilitate deeper self-understanding and to promote behavior change (Sperry, 2008).

This approach favors a therapeutic relationship that is cooperative, empathic, and non-dogmatic. Based on the family constellation and early recollections, and informed by an Adlerian case conceptualization, treatment is planned in line with specific goals and is tailored around the client's readiness for change. Interventions and techniques are chosen from Adlerian and other approaches. Through respectful dialogue and encouragement, clients are challenged to correct mistaken lifestyle convictions and change behavior. In short, Adlerian therapy is a therapeutic approach that is positive, flexible, and culturally and ethically sensitive.

References

Ansbacher, H. L., & Ansbacher, R. R. (Eds.). (1956). *The individual psychology of Alfred Adler.* New York, NY: Harper & Row.

Arcineiga, G., & Newlon, B. (2003). Counseling and psychotherapy: Multicultural considerations. In D. Capuzz & D. Gross (Eds.). *Counseling and psychotherapy: Theories and interventions* (3rd ed.) (pp. 417–441). Upper Saddle River, NJ. Merrill/Prentice Hall.

Carlson, J., & Englar-Carlson, M. (2017). *Adlerian psychotherapy.* Washington DC: American Psychological Association.

Carlson, J., Watts, R., & Maniacci, M. (2006). *Adlerian therapy: Theory and practice.* Washington DC: American Psychological Association.

Clark, A. J. (2002). *Early recollections: Theory and practice in counseling and psychotherapy.* New York, NY: Brunner-Routledge.

Dreikurs, R. (1967). *Psychodynamics, psychotherapy, and counseling: The collected papers of Rudolf Dreikurs, M.D.* Chicago, IL: The Alfred Adler Institute.

Mosak, H. H, & Di Pietro, R. (2006). *Early recollections: Interpretative method and application.* New York, NY: Routledge.

Mosak, H. H., & Maniacci, M. (1999). *A primer of Adlerian psychology.* New York, NY: Brunner-Routledge.

Mosak, H. H., & Maniacci, M. (1998). *Tactics in counseling and psychotherapy.* Itasca, IL: F. E. Peacock.

Sperry, L. (2018). Achieving evidence-based status for Adlerian therapy: Why it is needed and how to accomplish it. *Journal of Individual Psychology, 74*(3), 247–264..

Sperry, L. (2015). Personality disorders. In L. Sperry, J. Carlson, J. Duba-Sauerheber, & J. Sperry (Eds.). *Psychopathology and psychotherapy: DSM-5 diagnosis, case conceptualization and treatment* (3rd ed.) (pp. 27–61). New York, NY: Routledge.

Sperry, L. (2010). *Highly effective therapy: Developing essential clinical competencies in counseling and psychotherapy.* New York, NY: Routledge.

Sperry, L. (2008). Adlerian psychotherapy. In K. Jordan (Ed.). *The quick theory reference guide: A resource for expert and novice mental health professionals* (pp. 23–29). New York, NY: Nova Science Publishers.

Sperry, L., & Sperry, J. (2012). *Case conceptualization: Mastering this competency with ease and confidence.* New York, NY: Routledge.

3

Adlerian Pattern-Focused Therapy

Learning Objectives

In this chapter, you will learn the following:

1. The evolving practice of Adlerian therapy
2. The origins, premises, and components of Adlerian pattern-focused therapy
3. The interventions and techniques of Adlerian pattern-focused therapy
4. Evidence-based practice and ethical consideration in Adlerian pattern-focused therapy
5. Practicing Adlerian pattern-focused therapy: The case of Jennifer.

Because the practice of conventional Adlerian therapy is typically eclectic, it provides therapists considerable flexibility in choosing and applying interventions from other approaches (Carlson, Watts, & Maniacci , 2006). The downside is that it has yet to be standardized and achieve evidence-based (EB) status. Accordingly, to achieve this status and continue to be reimbursable, a version of it has been developed. It is called Adlerian pattern-focused therapy.

This chapter begins with a brief discussion of the evolving practice of Adlerian therapy. It then describes the origins and components of Adlerian pattern-focused therapy. Since pattern is the key component of this approach, the section on pattern is extensive. Next, its core therapeutic strategy is discussed. This is followed by a description of the most common interventions and techniques of Adlerian patter-focused therapy. Then, the characteristic structure to therapeutic process and specific session is described. Finally, a case example illustrates the discussion.

The Evolving Practice of Adlerian Therapy

My (LS) lifelong involvement with Adlerian therapy began in graduate school and continued in the psychotherapy certificate program at the Adler Institute of Chicago (now Adler University). There I had the great fortune of being involved in group supervision with Rudolf Dreikurs, M.D. in his practice. Beginning in the late 1960s, Adlerian training proliferated throughout North America and the world. Adlerian therapy would also be recognized as among the top three best therapy approaches, based on meta-analysis of nearly 400 psychotherapy research studies (Smith & Glass, 1977).

However, things began to change rather dramatically in the late 1980s when the accountability movement arrived and championed evidence-based treatment. Since then, all major therapeutic approaches have faced the choice of achieving evidence-based status or becoming historical footnotes. It is becoming a liability for approaches not to be recognized as evidence based. Until now, Adlerian therapy has not been so recognized. Furthermore, while it has a recognizable assessment strategy of lifestyle assessment, it had not developed a unique therapeutic strategy, which is essential in achieving evidence-based status. Accordingly, Adlerian pattern-focused therapy was developed with a defined core therapeutic strategy and other requisites of this status.

Origins and Premises of Adlerian Pattern-Focused Therapy

This section describes the origins, premises, and components of Adlerian pattern-focused therapy.

Origins

Adlerian pattern-focused therapy has its origins in Adlerian therapy as well as in biopsychosocial therapy and psychotherapy outcomes research. Because the theory and practice of Adlerian therapy has already been described in chapters 1 and 2, the following paragraphs focus on biopsychosocial therapy and psychotherapy outcomes research.

Biopsychosocial therapy is an integrative approach that incorporates biological, psychological, and socio-cultural factors, which emphasize a therapeutic process that focuses on pattern identification, pattern change, and pattern maintenance (Sperry, 1988, 2000, 2006). Part of the utility of this approach is its integrative nature but applying this from an Adlerian perspective provides the ability to assess for more specified patterns. Pattern and pattern recognition will be elaborated on further in following sections.

Psychotherapy outcomes research assesses and evaluates the effectiveness of psychotherapy and the mechanisms of change associated with treatments for psychological disorders. It also involves monitoring treatment progress and the therapeutic over the course of therapy (Sperry, Brill, Howard, & Grissom, 1996; Sperry 2010). Outcomes research is an integral part of identifying the evidence basis for an approach, and I (LS) have been engaged in outcomes research throughout my professional career.

Premises

Adlerian pattern-focused therapy is based on four premises. The first premise is that individuals unwittingly develop a self-perpetuating, maladaptive pattern of functioning and relating to others. Subsequently, this pattern underlies a client's presenting issues. The second premise is that pattern change (i.e., replacement or shifting to a more adaptive pattern) is a necessary component of evidence-based practice. The third premise is that effective treatment involves a change process in which the client and therapist collaborate to identify the maladaptive pattern, break it, and replace it with a more adaptive pattern. At least two outcomes have been observed to result from this change process: increased well-being as well as resolution of the patient/client's presenting issue (Sperry & Sperry, 2012). Finally, the fourth premise is that the process of replacing non-productive thinking and behaviors with more adaptive or productive ones can more quickly lead to effective therapeutic change. This contrasts with therapeutic approaches that attempt to directly restructure or challenge cognitions (i.e., cognitive therapy, or to directly modify behavior, behavior therapy).

Components of Adlerian Pattern-Focused Therapy

Components refers to the core elements and active ingredients of a therapeutic approach that effect change. Adlerian pattern-focused therapy involves four such components: lifestyle and patterns, the core therapeutic strategy of replacement, Adlerian and other treatment interventions and techniques, and outcomes monitoring and evaluation.

1. Lifestyle and Pattern

Assessment of the lifestyle was introduced in chapter 2. Adlerian pattern-focused therapy identifies the core component of pattern as synonymous with life strategy in lifestyle assessment, particularly in this syllogism: self-view, world view, and life strategy. Lifestyle, style of life, and life strategy are different ways of referring to an individual's pattern of thinking, feeling, and acting. Identifying and shifting or replacing a maladaptive pattern to a more adaptive one is the heart of Adlerian pattern-focused therapy. A succinct statement of a pattern would follow the outline "I am, ... " "Life/ others/ the world is, ..." "Therefore, I...." For example, "I am inferior, and life is dangerous; therefore, I must withdraw to protect myself." The "therefore" statement is the individual's life strategy or basic pattern. Once identified, this pattern serves as a concise case conceptualization that can drive treatment decisions for replacing the maladaptive pattern with one more adaptive or flexible.

Pattern Identification

One unique element of Adlerian pattern-focused therapy is pattern identification. The therapist determines the client's pattern, with feedback from the client, using information provided in the assessment interview, as well as early interpretations and Adlerian lifestyle factors. Clients may exhibit more than one pattern and maladaptive responses may range in severity.

TABLE 3.1 Key Concepts

Presentation: The individual's presenting problem (i.e., symptom or conflict). Typically, it is a response to a precipitant that is congruent with the client's pattern

Precipitant: Triggers that activate the client's pattern, leading to the presenting problem

Predisposition: Factors that foster and lead to either maladaptive or adaptive patterns

Pattern: The predicable, consistent, and self-perpetuating style and way individuals think, feel, act, cope, and defend themselves

Perpetuants: Factors that maintain the presenting problem and pattern

Accurate client pattern identification is essential to effective delivery of Adlerian pattern-focused therapy.

The pattern can be identified after eliciting the presentation, precipitants, perpetuates, and predispositions. Table 3.1 defines these terms.

It is critical to note that maladaptive pattern and adaptive pattern rather consistently reflect an individual's core personality dynamics. Accordingly, it can be helpful for therapists to identify an individual's basic personality style or personality disorder. Then, the therapists can develop hypotheses about corresponding maladaptive patterns. It is important to specify a corresponding adaptive pattern since this will be reflected in the second order treatment goal.

These hypotheses can be checked against the common patterns associated with specific personality styles and disorders. Table 3.2 is a resource of common maladaptive and adaptive patterns based on personality dynamics.

Examples of Pattern Recognition

The first example of Adlerian pattern recognition is in the case of Geri (Sperry, 2015). This client presented with depression and an avoidant personality disorder style. As it was derived from her early recollections, her lifestyle syllogism was "I am inadequate and defective"; "Life is demanding, arbitrary, and unsafe"; "Therefore avoid relationships and withdraw when feeling unsafe" (p. 22). Her life strategy is a common theme amongst individuals with an avoidant personality, but the specific language and use of lifestyle analysis allows for a concise, personal, and collaborative core conceptualization from which both the client and clinician can work. It should be noted that her life strategy is consistent with her observed maladaptive pattern of "feels safe by avoiding others." Furthermore, her maladaptive pattern and life strategy informed how treatment was subsequently focused. The client presented for social isolation and depressive symptoms, and by replacing this maladaptive pattern with a more adaptive one, these issues (among others) were resolved (Sperry, 2015).

The second example involves a secondary pattern. While a single maladaptive pattern is the most common presentation, occasionally clients also present with a secondary pattern, which can confuse the therapists and complicate the treatment process. Recognizing this secondary pattern is necessary in reducing confusion and effecting therapeutic change. The case of Aimee is a useful example of this double pattern. Originally, part of an American Psychological Association six session video series with Jon Carlson as the therapist, this case was later transcribed

TABLE 3.2 Guide to Personality and Pattern Identification

Personality style or disorder	Likely adaptive [A] pattern and maladaptive [M] pattern
Histrionic	[A] Gets attention and feels worthwhile [M] Gets attention, but pays a high price and/or becomes compromised
Dependent	[A] Pleases others by meeting their needs and meets one's own needs [M] Pleases others by meeting their needs but does not meet one's own
Narcissistic	[A] Self-confident and respectful of others [M] Elevates self but uses and/or belittles others
Paranoid	[A] Sizes up and is careful in relating to others [M] Sizes up but expects to be harmed by others
Antisocial	[A] Lives by one's own internal code and is law abiding [M] Lives by one's own internal code but is not law abiding
Avoidant	[A] Feels safe and safely connects with some others [M] Feels safe but avoids (isolates/disconnects) most others
Schizoid	[A] Limited need for companionship and more comfortable alone [M] Limited need for companionship but actively avoids others
Schizotypal	[A] Indifferent to social convention and relates with familiar people [M] Indifferent to social convention but wary of unfamiliar people
Obsessive compulsive	[A] Reasonably conscientious and somewhat emotionally close [M] Overly conscientious/perfectionistic but emotionally distant
Passive aggressive	[A] Agrees to do what is expected and will do that, albeit hesitantly [M] Agrees to do what is expected but will make excuses and not do it
Borderline	Pattern reflects the decompensated version of the underlying personality (dependent, histrionic, or passive aggressive)

and analyzed (Sperry & Carlson, 2014). Her primary maladaptive pattern was observed to be care for others but not care for herself. Her secondary pattern was to strive to be perfect with her over-conscientiousness. Based on her early recollections, her life strategy was "Therefore, be conscientious in taking care of and pleasing others." This life strategy confirms the maladaptive patterns and vice versa. Through a brief course of effective psychotherapy, Aimee was able to replace these maladaptive patterns with more adaptive ones, while also resolving her presenting concerns (Sperry & Carlson, 2014).

Pattern Shifting

A second unique element is pattern shifting by means of the query sequence (i.e., a strategy for processing therapeutic material). Shifting from a maladaptive to a more adaptive pattern indicates that second order change has occurred. Cognitive Behavior Analysis System of Psychotherapy (CBASP) and Adlerian pattern-focused therapy offer options for making that shift.

Recognized as an evidence-based or empirically supported treatment by the American Psychological Association (APA, 2018), cognitive behavior analysis system of psychotherapy (CBASP) was developed by James P. McCullough for the treatment of chronic depression (McCullough, 2000). While CBASP fosters consequential thinking and replacement of problematic thoughts and behaviors, it does not identify pattern nor analyze pattern-laden situations. Accordingly, the most it can achieve is symptoms resolution, or personal or relationship stabilization, which are first order change goals.

In contrast, because its focus also includes pattern shifting, Adlerian pattern-focused therapy can also achieve second order change goals. One of the most important reasons for emphasizing the life strategy in Adlerian pattern-focused therapy is that this focus increases the applicability of to a much broader range of clients and indications than many other therapeutic approaches. Having a strong conceptualization of a client allows for strong explanatory and predictive power (Sperry & Sperry, 2012). Also, understanding pattern from an Adlerian perspective can provide an integrative approach to a host of clinical presentations (Sperry, 2015). Even at a lesser emotional or cognitive developmental level, clients can benefit from Adlerian pattern-focused therapy. Approaches that focus on changing or modifying self-other schemas (i.e., self-view and world view), and that emphasize interpretation, cognitive disputation, or restructuring, require a much higher level of cognitive emotional development. This limits the potential benefit of many of these approaches with a presentation such as depression, in which clients often have lower developmental functioning in these areas.

2. Replacement Strategy

Replacement is one of the core therapeutic strategies that is identified with a particular approach. For example, interpretation is the core strategy in psychoanalysis, while cognitive restructuring is the core strategy in cognitive therapy, and exposure in behavior therapy. In contrast, replacement is the core therapeutic strategy in narrative therapy (White & Epston, 1990), cognitive behavioral analysis system of psychotherapy (McCullough, 2000), and reality therapy (Glasser, 1975). All three utilize a core strategy of replacing hurtful thoughts and behaviors with healthier, more helpful ones. Many therapists use replacement as an adjunctive strategy when there is insufficient time to process a new issue using interpretation or cognitive disputation. For example, when the client is depressed or distressed about not having a friend to hang with on a Saturday evening, the client may choose to lie in bed and think about not having anything to do. The therapist encourages the client to generate replacement behaviors (call a specific friend) or a replacement thought ("When I call my friends, I know that people want to spend time with me").

Since Adlerian therapy does not currently possess a unique or signature core therapeutic strategy, the replacement strategy was adopted for Adlerian pattern-focused therapy. A basic assumption is that thoughts and behaviors in specific situations most likely reflect the individual's overall life strategy or pattern. To the extent to which that pattern is maladaptive, relief and resolution occur when that maladaptive pattern—and its associated hurtful thoughts and behaviors—are replaced with a more adaptive pattern.

3. Interventions and Techniques of Adlerian Pattern-Focused Therapy

This section describes the interventions and techniques that characterize Adlerian pattern-focused therapy. They include the query strategy and six Adlerian techniques: encouragement, acting "as if," reflecting "as if," push button, task setting, and roleplaying.

Query Sequence

The query sequence is a major change intervention of Adlerian pattern-focused therapy. This questioning sequence was adapted from CBASP. As noted earlier, the core therapeutic strategy of CBASP is replacement, and so it is not surprising that the query sequence is a replacement intervention. As such, it focuses on identifying and replacing hurtful thoughts and behaviors with more helpful ones. It consists of two phases: the situation analysis phase with six steps, and the remediation phase with two additional steps (McCullough, Schramm & Penberthy, 2014). The genius of this approach is that it is relatively easy to learn and apply to a wide variety of difficult client presentations. In the process of analyzing a specific situation together, clients can "replace" problematic and hurtful thoughts and behaviors with more helpful ones. This often occurs more quickly than if the therapeutic core strategy was to cognitively restructure problematic thoughts or to modify problematic behaviors. As the expectation and demand for therapy become shorter and time limited, there is considerable value in replacement approaches like CBASP.

To increase its teachability, the CBASP therapeutic process was refashioned to nine steps (Sperry, 2006), and building on its strategy of replacement, an Adlerian and pattern-focused emphasis became a key component of Adlerian pattern-focused therapy (Sperry, 2018).

To increase the likelihood of clinical success, a 10th step was added. It includes two key questions for rating and scaling therapeutic progress. The first assesses the "importance" of a making a specific change, while the second assesses the client's degree of "confidence" in achieving that change. Both are derived from motivational interviewing (Miller & Rollnick, 2012). The reader will find a more detailed account of the query sequence and Adlerian pattern-focused therapy in its treatment manual (Sperry & Bienstzok, 2018).

Query Sequence in Action

Briefly, here is how the 10-step query sequence is implemented. It focuses on analyzing and processing problematic situations. Invariably, these situations reflect the client's maladaptive pattern. Clients are first asked to describe the situation (1) and their associated thoughts (2) and behaviors (3). Then, they are asked to provide their desired or expected outcome in that situation (4) as well as the actual outcome (5). As clients typically report that they did not achieve their desired outcome (6), they are asked if they would like to review the situation and how it might have turned out differently (7). Assuming they are receptive, they are asked, one by one, if the thought helped or hurt them in achieving what they wanted in the situation (8). Typically, they were hurtful, so clients are asked what alternative thought would have been more helpful and how those alternatives would have helped them achieve the desired outcome. The reported behaviors are then analyzed in the same way, regarding whether they helped or hurt the client in achieving the desired outcome and which behaviors would have been more helpful (9), and then if their behaviors helped or hurt them in achieving that outcome (9). Finally, they are queried about the importance of shifting to more adaptive patterns and their confidence in achieving this (10).

A marker of therapeutic change is that clients find they achieve their desired or expected outcomes more often because of replacing a hurtful thought or behavior with a more helpful one, while at the same time incrementally replacing their maladaptive pattern with a more adaptive one. As therapy progresses, clients come to understand how their thoughts and behaviors reflect their maladaptive pattern as well as activate symptoms and account for reduced functioning.

Encouragement

Encouragement "refers to the process of increasing one's courage in order to face the difficulties of life" (Carlson & Englar-Carlson, 2017, p. 29). Without encouragement, individuals are unlikely to have faith in themselves, expect that their lives will improve, or that they will function better. Encouragement has significant implications for therapy. Because they view individuals from a growth and well-being model rather than a pathology model, Adlerian therapists view clients as discouraged rather than sick. That means clients present for therapy because they are discouraged and lack the courage and confidence to deal effectively with life's challenges. Accordingly, Adlerian therapy emphasizes encouragement. In fact, encouragement is the fundamental ingredient of therapeutic change for Adlerian therapists.

Encouragement is not just a technique, but an attitude and way of life. It is "the process of helping clients to feel that they have worth as they are. It is shown when therapists demonstrate social interest to and for their clients" (Carlson & Englar-Carlson, 2017, p. 141). That means that therapists show confidence in their clients' strengths and abilities. It means that they identify and draw on the client's past successes, and that they support the clients' efforts and treatment progress. In fact, therapeutic success is largely dependent on the therapist's "'ability to provide encouragement' and that failure generally occurred 'due to the inability of the therapy to encourage'" (Carlson et al., 2006, p. 74).

Acting "As If"

The Adlerian technique of acting "as if" is a key intervention technique in Adlerian pattern-focused therapy (Carlson et al., 2006; Mosak & Maniacci, 1998). It involves asking clients to begin acting as if they were already the way they would like to be (e.g., more confident, independent, or caring). In other words, they **replace** a less healthy behavior with a healthier one. Several variants of this technique are described (Carich, 1997).

Behavioral Activation

An acting "as if" variant is behavioral activation, which is an intervention for breaking the cycles of inactivity and avoidance common in disorders such as depression (Dimaggio & Shahar, 2017). For example, depressed individuals characteristically limit their activities to avoid unwanted thoughts and feelings. This results in less positive reinforcement and reward from pleasant activities and an increase in symptoms. They are likely to avoid necessary tasks and withdraw from others. This results in feelings of defeat, hopelessness, and disconnection from others. While behavioral activation was initially employed in cognitive behavior therapy, it has been utilized with many therapeutic approaches and most clinical conditions. Not surprisingly, behavioral activation is quite compatible with Adlerian therapy.

Reflecting "As If"

The reflecting "as if" technique (Watts, 2003) extends the acting "as if" technique. It asks clients to take a reflective step back prior to stepping forward to "act as if." It encourages them to reflect on and **replace** how life would be different if they were acting the way they desired. It includes the following elements: collaborative goal setting and brainstorming, measurable behaviors, and behavioral planning. Instead of interpretation, cognitive restructuring, or exposure, the client simply replaces one way of thinking about himself or herself with another.

Push Button Technique

The push button technique, which was specifically developed as an Adlerian intervention for depression (Mosak & Maniacci, 1998), involves clients being asked to concentrate first on a pleasant experience and the feelings it generates, and then on an unpleasant experience. Clients recognize that they can take control of their emotional responses by simply "pushing the button" to **replace** negative experience or feeling state. It is a particularly effective technique for interrupting depressive symptoms. Instead of the lengthy process of interpretation or cognitive restructuring, the client simply replaces one feeling state with another. The client is encouraged to concentrate on pleasant experiences and the feelings associated with them and practice pushing that button.

Task Setting

Task setting is an Adlerian technique that encourages clients to assume responsibility for themselves and how their behavior impacts others. It is a form of homework (Mosak & Maniacci, 1998). In dealing with depressed individuals, Adler (1958) advised: "You can be cured in fourteen days if you follow this prescription. Try to think every day of how you can please someone" (p. 258). And later, "All my efforts are devoted toward increasing the social interest of the patients.... As soon as he can connect himself with his fellow man on an equal and cooperative footing, he is cured" (p. 260). Another example is to give a student procrastinating in writing his or her doctoral dissertation the task of writing 250 words each day.

The therapist assigns tasks that can be performed inside or outside the therapy room. The task should be "relatively simple and set at a level at which patients may be able to sabotage the task but are less likely to fail and then scold the therapist" (Mosak & Maniacci, 1998, p. 119). This powerful technique **replaces** self-interested behavior with social interest behavior. In place of complicated interventions such as cognitive disputation or systematic desensitization, the clients simply replace one way of thinking about themselves with another.

In short, the core strategy of replacement is quite compatible with Adlerian therapy practice. It is also the mechanism of change associated with these four Adlerian techniques.

Role Playing

Role playing is another variant of the "as if" technique (Carich, 1997). It is also known as behavioral rehearsal. In this commonly used intervention, the therapist helps the client put him- herself into an anticipated role or situation, giving the client an opportunity to practice dialog and behaviors. For example, the client may practice newly learned social skills with the therapist to master them and build confidence before engaging in a social interaction outside therapy. The therapist can play the role of the individual the client is practicing interacting with, or model for the client how the client might more effectively interact with that individual. In Adlerian pattern-focused therapy, role playing is used as a way for clients to experience and practice tasks they may have had trouble with in the past.

4. Outcome Evaluation and Monitoring

The final component in Adlerian pattern-focused therapy is the use of assessment measures to monitor progress throughout therapy. These measures include the Patient Health Questionnaire-9 (PHQ-9), the Social Interest Index-Short Form, and early recollections (ERs). ERs are collected at the first and last session. This second set of ERs can provide progress on the second treatment goal as well as on changes in social interest. The PHQ-9 and SII-SF are introduced here and illustrated in the case of Jennifer in subsequent chapters.

Patient Health Questionnaire-9

The Patient Health Questionnaire-9 (PHQ-9) (Kroenke & Spitzer, 2002) is a nine-item measure of depression that reflects the DSM-5 criteria for major depressive disorder (American Psychiatric Association, 2013). It is commonly used as a quick screener for depression in both medical settings as well as psychiatric settings. Ratings are collected at the beginning of each session and are an effective way of monitoring treatment. They reflect progress on the first treatment goal, which is symptom reduction.

Social Interest Index-Short Form

The Social Interest Index-Short Form (SII-SF) is a short measure of social interest. The SII-SF (Leak, 2006) is a revised and shortened version of the Social Interest Index (SII) and is considered the most frequently used and most valid measure of social interest (Bass, Curlette, Kern, & McWilliams, 2002). Changes in social interest scores presumably reflect both a shift from a maladaptive to a more adaptive pattern, as well as changes in the ERs over the course of therapy. The SII-SF is collected pre- and post-therapy and at the mid-point of treatment.

Client progress is also monitored using the Outcome Rating Scale (ORS) (Miller & Duncan, 2002), while the quality of the therapeutic relationship is continuously assessed using the Session Rating Scale (SRS) (Duncan, et al., 2003). The ORS is used to track individual, social, and interpersonal outcomes over the course of therapy, while the quality of the therapeutic relationship is continuously assessed using the SRS. These and other self-report measures are used in the case of Jennifer and will be described in more detail in chapter 5.

Adlerian Pattern-Focused Therapy: Session Structure

After identifying the four basic components of Adlerian pattern-focused therapy, let's now turn to how the therapy process is structured in terms of specific sessions.

The case of Jennifer is a completed therapy, which was planned for 10 sessions of individual therapy utilizing Adlerian pattern-focused therapy. While this approach is well suited for brief, time-limited therapy, the number of sessions could be longer or shorter. Table 3. 3 summarizes the structure and content of the 10 sessions.

Evidence-Based Practice and Adlerian Pattern-Focused Therapy

Trainees and practicing therapists are increasingly interested in evidence-based practice and evidence-based approaches. These two are related but different. Let's begin with evidence-based practice.

In the recent past, it was common for therapists to make treatment decisions based on the therapeutic orientation they espoused and their experience. Less often, their decisions were based on scientific evidence that the treatment they provided would be safe, effective, and ethical. Today, because of the increasing requirement for accountability, there has been a shift to the concept of evidence-based practice. As first described, evidence-based practice is a process of inquiry for helping therapists and their clients make key decisions about treatment. It is a strategy for deciding which interventions to provide based on the following factors: research evidence, clinician experience and expertise, client preferences and values, plus professional ethics, situational circumstances, and the availability of resources (Sackett, Richardson, Rosenberg, Haynes, & Brian, 1997).

TABLE 3.3 Capsule Summary of Sessions One Through Ten

Session 1: Complete a diagnostic evaluation re: any DSM-5 symptom and/or personality disorder. Identify client's presumptive maladaptive pattern, elicit at least two to three early recollections, and give first administrations PHQ-9 and SII-SF. Socialize client in this therapeutic approach, explain treatment protocol, and secure full informed consent. Establish first and second order treatment goals and mutually agree on homework.

Session 2: Administer PHQ-9 and ORS immediately prior to session. Discuss scores on PHQ-9 and ORS and review homework. Mutually agree on the maladaptive pattern and the need to shift to a more adaptive pattern. Process problematic situations using the APFT query. Introduce behavioral activation/acting as if exercise and how to log and rate the scheduled activities. Mutually agree on homework. Administer and discuss SRS.

Session 3–9: Administer PHQ-9 and ORS immediately prior to session. Discuss scores on PHQ-9, ORS, and mood scale and review homework. Process problematic situations using the APFT query re: maladaptive pattern. Describe additional interventions, such as push button technique, as indicated. Mutually agree on homework. Administer and discuss SRS.

Session 10: Administer PHQ-9, SII-SF, and ORS immediately prior to session. Focus of session is on termination, so begin by reviewing PHQ-9 and ORS and then progress on attainment of first order change goals (from Session 1). Next, elicit at least two to three ERs. Then, review progress toward the second order change goal, evident by changes in ERs reflecting a more adaptive pattern. A relapse prevention plan is established. Discuss what the client identifies as other issues to work on their own (third order change goals), specify options for follow-up afterwards.

It is important to note that evidence-based practice is different from an evidence-based approach or intervention, which is also known as "empirically supported treatment" (APA Presidential Task Force on Evidence-Based Practice, 2006; American Psychological Association, 2018). That means that one can provide an empirically supported treatment *without* considering the factors of client values and clinician expertise. Another way of saying this is that engaging in evidence-based practice is more encompassing and demanding than simply employing an evidence-based approach or intervention. More specifically, it means that a therapist may engage in evidence-based practice with or without employing an evidence-based approach or intervention.

Adlerian pattern-focused therapy is not yet listed by Division 12 of the American Psychological Association (2018) as one of its 80 empirically supported treatments. However, a key component of Adlerian pattern-focused therapy, CBASP, is recognized as an empirically supported treatment by the American Psychological Association. Accordingly, Adlerian pattern-focused therapy can be considered an evidence-informed therapy approach because it incorporates this key component.

Finally, a therapist or trainee can confidently engage in the evidence-based practice of Adlerian pattern-focused therapy, assuming that the therapist has sufficient expertise to match client values and then provide a treatment approach supported by sufficient research evidence. At this point in time, and because a key component of it is empirically supported, Adlerian pattern-focused therapy appears to have more value in evidence-based practice than conventional Adlerian therapy.

Ethical Considerations and Adlerian Pattern-Focused Therapy Practice

Trainees and practicing therapists are also interested in the ethics of practicing specific therapy approaches. Major ethical concerns are that a therapy approach is both safe and effective. In general, "[t]he ethics of risk and benefit indicate that treatments with strong scientific evidence for efficacy and safety offer significant ethical advantages over therapies which do not have such an evidence base" (Sookman, 2015, p. 1295). It is noteworthy that Adlerian pattern-focused therapy does offer this ethical advantage since its core therapeutic strategy does possess evidence of both efficacy and safety. In particular, a psychotherapeutic approach should also be evaluated with regard to specific areas of ethical evidence-based practice. These areas include the client-therapist relationship, involvement in the therapeutic process, informed consent, psychoeducation, homework, and disorder-specific approaches (Sookman, 2015). To the extent that these criteria are met, the basic ethical principle is fostered: "The primary responsibility of counselors is to respect the dignity and promote the welfare of clients" (American Counseling Association, 2014, p. 2).

Here is a brief evaluation of these areas or criteria in Adlerian pattern-focused therapy. A hallmark of this approach is cooperation and collaboration in both the client-therapist relationship and in involvement of the client in the therapeutic process. The purpose of psychoeducation and other in-session activities is to grow by learning new attitudes and skills, which the client has agreed are necessary. Similarly, homework, or between-session activities, are mutually agreed-on activities that foster growth and empowerment. These include acting "as if," reflecting "as if," role playing and the push button technique. As demonstrated in the transcriptions of the Case of Jennifer (in chapters 3–9), informed consent is an ongoing process. In line with the basic ethical principle, respect is continually accorded clients while their welfare and well-being are fostered. Finally, because a key component of Adlerian pattern-focused therapy has achieved evidence-based status for its efficacy in the treatment of major depressive disorder, it meets the criteria of a disorder-specific approach in that the main case in this book involves this disorder.

Adlerian Pattern-Focused Therapy: Illustrative Case of Jennifer

The following case example summarizes the application of Adlerian pattern-focused therapy in a planned, 10-session therapy with a client who presents with major depressive disorder. She was referred by her physician for psychotherapy because she did not want to take medication for her depressive symptoms. She was particularly concerned about medication side effects, although she was receptive to the addition of medication if her symptoms were not sufficiently responsive to psychotherapy.

Background

Jennifer is a 21-year-old college student who presents with low mood, reduced pleasure, decreased motivation, and limited social interaction. Reportedly, these symptoms began three weeks ago, and this is the first time she has felt this down. She reports that increasing pressures and deadlines in her college courses have caused her stress and led her to isolate herself from her peers in order to keep up with her responsibilities. She is too embarrassed to talk to her parents about these because she doesn't want to disappoint them. She also reports being fatigued more quickly than usual and worries that this may ruin a future career as a lawyer. This has led her to feel undue guilt about her recent mood and performance in school. She is in her sophomore year of college and participates in numerous organized school events including the softball team and several study groups. She majors in pre-law and maintains a 3.9 GPA and works part time at a campus convenience store.

Diagnostic Impression

Jennifer meets six of nine DSM criteria for 269.22 major depressive disorder (moderate), single episode (American Psychiatric Association, 2013). She also displays an obsessive-compulsive personality style, missing the diagnosis of Obsessive-Compulsive Personality Disorder by one criteria. Jennifer was administered the Patient Health Questionnaire–9 (PHQ-9), on which she scored a 13, indicating moderate depression.

Family Constellation

Jennifer is the oldest of three children, each two years apart. She described that her parents often compared her siblings to her as though she was the standard that they were to aspire to, but also that they held very high standards for her. She was expected to maintain high grades and excel at multiple extracurricular activities. She described herself as being more like her father who is described as successful and perfectionistic. Her siblings are described as "Okay, but a nuisance sometimes." Her parents are described as having a good relationship and that her father was the primary breadwinner. She stated her parents could be critical of one another, with her father criticizing her mother's "lack of time-management skills," and her mother primarily criticizing her father's dedication to his work. She added that her parents never seemed to work out these conflicts and mostly just avoided talking about them. Her family appears to value achievement and success. Accordingly, she was expected to go to college and go into either business, law, or medicine. She stated she has always been the most athletic of her siblings and received the best grades. It appears she has a complex relationship with her youngest sibling, vacillating between envying her because "she's so laid back—doesn't have a care in the world," and being annoyed with her because "she's clueless."

Early Recollections

As already noted, early recollections are recalled stories of single, specific incidents from childhood and are central in an Adlerian assessment, ER pre-therapy, as well as in monitoring therapy outcomes, ER post-therapy (Clark, (2002).

ER: Pre-Therapy

Two recollections were reported in the first session. The first ER occurred at age six: She said: "I spent several hours a day over the course of a week building a tall tower with toy bricks. I came home from school the next day to find that my little sister had knocked it down. I pushed her down and my parents punished me by taking a privilege away from me." The most vivid part was "seeing my tower all over the floor." She reports feeling upset and angry but didn't show it. She thought: "It's ruined. My sister makes trouble for me and I get punished. It's not fair."

The second recollection occurred at age eight. She said: "I was playing my violin solo at our school's music recital and I made two small mistakes. Afterwards, my parents yelled at me for not practicing enough. The most vivid part was "making those mistakes." She reports feeling "embarrassed, sad, and worried." She thought: "I worked so hard and I failed. I can't stand it."

ER Interpretation

Jennifer's early recollections are consistent with her obsessive-compulsive pattern of achievement, perfectionism, and over-conscientiousness. In the first recollection, her hard work is "ruined" and she is punished for "moving against" her sister. The second recollection may foreshadow her depressive response to overly high demands and lack of emotional support from others. This is consistent with and confirms the therapist's observed maladaptive pattern of over-conscientiousness and perfectionistic striving that interferes with completing tasks.

Case Conceptualization

Jennifer presents for treatment with major depression as noted by low mood, reduced pleasure, decreased motivation, and guilt about school performance. These symptoms and decreased function appear to be precipitated by social isolation after increased focus on academics. Her maladaptive pattern is one of over-conscientiousness and perfectionism to the point of impaired effectiveness. Likely predisposing factors include the following: Biologically, her symptoms may reflect a genetic vulnerability to depression as her maternal uncle had been diagnosed and treated for depression with medication. Psychologically, her personality style is notably for obsessive-compulsive features. Her self-other schema includes a self-view of "I am responsible for doing things right and not making mistakes" and a world-view of "Life is demanding and unfair. Things can go wrong if you don't pay attention to details." Her life strategy seems to be "I have to work hard, meet high expectations, and strive to be perfect." Skill deficits have also been identified. These include limited ability to cope with stressors and ineffective time management. Socially, Jennifer's history is notable for social isolation, high parental expectations for achievement, and difficulty getting along with siblings. Finally, perpetuants for her maladaptive pattern include social isolation, unreasonable self-expectations, high demands of her college courses, and guilt about failure to meet expectations. Culturally, she identifies as a White, middle-class Euro American who is highly acculturated. She explains her current symptoms as stress induced and believes that she is best treated with psychotherapy without medications. Treatment goals of first order change involve reducing depressive symptoms and increasing social connectedness (i.e., belonging). The second order change goal will involve shifting to a more adaptive pattern characterized by reasonable consciousness and reasonable effectiveness. Given her obsessive pattern it might be predicted that she will be overly talkative and resist getting in touch with "soft" affects. She might also experience ambivalence about termination. Prognosis for achieving treatment goals is good.

Concluding Note

The practice of Adlerian therapy has had a storied past and in the form of Adlerian pattern-focused therapy, its future looks bright. This standardized approach is easily learned and effectively practiced by both novice and experienced therapists. Since 2012, this version of Adlerian therapy has been fully implemented in a graduate psychotherapy training program (Sperry, 2016; Sperry & Sperry, 2018), and initial data shows it to be effective and successful in achieving treatment goals in clients. Furthermore, because it incorporates a key component of a recognized empirically supported (evidence-based) treatment, Adlerian pattern-focused therapy can be considered an evidence-informed therapy approach.

Chapters 4 through 9 focus on the practice of Adlerian pattern-focused therapy in a completed, 10-session therapy with a client, Jennifer, who presents with a major mental disorder.

References

Adler, A. (1958). *What life should mean to you*. New York, NY: Capricorn.

American Counseling Association (2014). *ACA code of ethics*. Alexandria, VA: Author.

American Psychiatric Association. (2013). *Diagnostic and statistical manual of mental disorders* (5th ed.). Arlington, VA: American Psychiatric Publishing.

American Psychological Association (2018). *Psychological treatments*. Retrieved from https://www.div12.org/treatments/

APA Presidential Task Force on Evidence-Based Practice (2006). Evidence-based practice in psychology. *American Psychologist, 61*(4), 271–85.

Bass, M. L., Curlette, W. L., Kern, R. M, & McWilliams, A. E. (2002). Social interest: A meta-analysis of a multidimensional construct. *Journal of Individual Psychology, 58*(1), 4–34.

Carich, M. (1997). Variations of the "as if" technique. In J. Carlson. & S. Slavik, (Eds.). (1997). *Techniques in Adlerian psychology*. (pp. 153–160). Washington DC: Accelerated Development.

Carlson, J., & Englar-Carlson, M. (2017). *Adlerian psychotherapy*. Washington DC: American Psychological Association.

Carlson, J., Watts, R. E., & Maniacci, M. (2006). *Adlerian therapy: Theory and process*. Washington DC: American Psychological Association.

Clark, A. (2002). *Early recollections: Theory and practice in counseling and psychotherapy*. New York, NY: Routledge.

Dimaggio, G., & Shahar, G. (2017). Behavioral activation as a common mechanism of change across different orientations and disorders. *Psychotherapy, 54*(3), 221–224.

Duncan, B., Miller, S., Parks, L., Claud, D., Reynolds, L., Brown, J., & Johnson, L. (2003). The Session Rating Scale. Preliminary properties of a "working" alliance measure. *Journal of Affective Disorders*, 49, 59–72.

Glasser, W. (1975). *Reality therapy: A new approach to psychiatry.* New York, NY: Harper & Row

Kroenke, K. & Spitzer, R. L. (2002). The PHQ-9: A new depression and diagnostic severity measure. *Psychiatric Annals*, 32(9), 509–521.

Leak, G. K. (2006). Development and validation of a revised measure of Adlerian social interest. *Social Behavior & Personality: An International Journal*, 34, 443–449.

McCullough, J. (2000). *Treatment for chronic depression: Cognitive behavioral analysis system of psychotherapy.* New York, NY: Guilford.

McCullough, J., Schramm, E., & Penberthy, K. (2014). *CBASP as a distinctive treatment for persistent depressive disorder: Distinctive features.* New York, NY: Routledge.

Miller, S., & Duncan, B. (2002). *The outcomes rating scale.* Chicago, IL: Author.

Miller, W., & Rollnick, S. (2002). *Motivational interviewing* (2nd ed.). New York, NY: Guilford.

Mosak, H. H., & Maniacci, M. (1998). *Tactics in counseling and psychotherapy.* Itasca, IL: F. E. Peacock.

Sackett, D., Richardson, W., Rosenberg, W., Haynes, R., & Brian, S. (21996). Evidence based medicine: What it is and what it isn't. *British Medical Journal*, 312(7023), 71–72.

Smith, M., & Glass, G. (1977). Meta-analysis of psychotherapy outcome studies. *American Psychologist*, 32(9), 752–760.

Sookman, D. (2015). Ethical practice of cognitive behavior therapy. In J. Sadler, B. Fulford, & C. Van Staden, (Ed.), *Oxford handbook of psychiatric ethics, Vol. 2.* (pp. 1293–1305). New York, NY: Oxford University Press.

Sperry, L. (2018). Achieving evidence-based status for Adlerian therapy: Why it is needed and how to accomplish it. *Journal of Individual Psychology*, 74(3), 247–264.

Sperry, L. (2016). Educating the next generation of psychotherapists: Considering the future of theory and practice in Adlerian psychotherapy. *Journal of Individual Psychology* 72(1), 4–11.

Sperry, L. (2015). Diagnosis, case conceptualization, and treatment. In L. Sperry, J. Carlson, J, Sauerheber, & J. Sperry. (Eds.) *Psychopathology and psychotherapy* (3rd ed.) (pp. 36–50) New York, NY: Routledge.

Sperry, L. (2006). *Psychological treatment of chronic illness: The biopsychosocial therapy approach.* New York, NY: Brunner/Mazel.

Sperry, L. (2000). Biopsychosocial therapy: Essential strategies and tactics. In J. Carlson & L. Sperry (Eds.). *Briefly therapy with individuals and couples.* Phoenix, AZ: Zeig, Tucker & Theisen.

Sperry, L. (1988). Biopsychosocial therapy: An integrative approach for tailoring treatment. *Journal of Individual Psychology*, 44, 225–235.

Sperry, L. & Binensztok, V. (2018). Adlerian pattern focused therapy: A treatment manual. *Journal of Individual Psychology*, 74(3), 309–348.

Sperry, L., Brill, P., Howard, K., & Grissom, G. (1996). *Treatment outcomes in psychotherapy and psychiatric interventions.* New York, NY: Brunner/Mazel.

Sperry, L., & Carlson, J. (2014). *How master therapists work: Effecting change from the first through the last session and beyond.* New York, NY: Routledge.

Sperry, J., & Sperry, L. (2018). *Cognitive behavior therapy in professional counseling practice.* New York, NY: Routledge.

Sperry, L., & Sperry, J. (2012). *Case conceptualization. Mastering this competency with ease and confidence.* New York, NY: Routledge. Sperry, J., & Sperry, L. (2018). *Cognitive behavior therapy in professional counseling practice.* New York, NY: Routledge.

Watkins, C. E. (1994). Measuring social interest. *Individual Psychology*, 50(1), 69–96.

Watts, R, (2003). Reflecting "as if": An integrative process in couples counseling. *The Family Journal*, 11(1), 73–75.

White, M., & Epston, D. (1990). *Narrative means to therapeutic ends.* New York, NY: Norton.

4

The Critical First Session

Learning Objectives

In this chapter, you will learn the following:

1. The key tasks of the first session of Adlerian pattern-focused therapy
2. The importance of and facilitating factors of the therapeutic alliance in APFT
3. How to complete the APFT assessment process, including pattern identification
4. How to identify both first and second order APFT treatment goals
5. A continuing case of how Adlerian pattern-focused therapy is practiced

The first session in Adlerian pattern-focused therapy is crucial for adequately assessing the client, as well as setting the stage for the rest of the therapy process. This process begins with establishing rapport and building the therapeutic alliance and continues with an integrative assessment, which involves completing a diagnostic evaluation, eliciting the client's family constellation and early recollections, and using very brief assessments, called screeners. The goal of this assessment is for the clinician to identify the client's lifestyle and maladaptive patterns, which are essential elements of the case conceptualization. The therapist socializes the client to the therapeutic approach and explains the treatment protocol. Both first and second order treatment goals are discussed and mutually agreed on with the client. Finally, the therapist must work to effect some change in the first session to build clinician credibility and increase the likelihood the client will continue in and be compliant with therapy.

This chapter will describe the first APFT session's key elements. Background information from the case of Jennifer is provided, followed by a full transcription of session 1, including commentary. There are several important tasks to be completed in the first session and Table 4.1 outlines them. Each will be elaborated on in subsequent sections.

TABLE 4.1 Key Tasks of the First Session

Securing informed consent: The client is informed about the nature of the treatment and of his or her rights and duties as a client.

Establishing the therapeutic alliance: The therapist builds the therapeutic alliance by joining with the client and creating an atmosphere that is mutual, safe, and nonjudgmental.

Conducting an assessment: The therapist completes an evaluation that includes the following:

- **Diagnostic evaluation:** A diagnostic evaluation is completed to make a diagnosis (if any), help identify the client's pattern, and rule out differential diagnoses and comorbidity.
- **Early recollections:** Two early recollections (before age eight) are elicited, including the most vivid part of the recollection and the client's thoughts and feelings at the time of the recalled event.
- **Family constellation:** The therapist assesses the client's birth order and family constellation.
- **Pattern identification:** The therapist identifies the client's maladaptive pattern, or lifestyle, through the diagnostic evaluation and early recollections. The therapist and client mutually agree on the maladaptive pattern.
- **Screeners:** Very brief instruments are used to assess the client's presenting problem and level of social interest, and later to monitor changes.

Socializing the client to treatment: The therapist should explain the treatment and protocol to the client, including how it is helpful and what is expected of the client.

Identifying treatment goals: The therapist and client agree on both first and second order goals. For the second order goal, the client should agree to the desired adaptive pattern.

Using motivational interviewing questions: The therapist assesses the client's level of motivation and confidence in changing the maladaptive pattern to a more adaptive one and engaging in the therapy process. This consists of two questions, regarding the level of importance and confidence about making specific change, for the client to rate on 0–10 a scale.

Effecting initial change: The therapist effects some change in the first session in order to increase clinician credibility (i.e., trust and confidence that change will occur) and instill hope by reframing the problem, using emotional first aid or other very brief interventions.

Assigning homework: The therapist assigns mutually agreed on homework for the client to begin keeping track of daily moods.

Securing Informed Consent

As in all therapeutic approaches, the client should be provided a statement outlining client rights and involvement in the therapeutic process and what to expect from treatment. This should outline confidentiality, fees, risks and benefits, the client's right to terminate therapy, and the nature of the treatment protocol. The client should be given the opportunity to address any questions before giving a signature of consent to treatment.

Because Jennifer was referred for psychotherapy by her physician because she did not want medication, it is important that the conditions for combined treatment (therapy plus medication) be discussed as part of informed consent process. In this discussion, they mutually agreed that if Jennifer's moods did not improve sufficiently by the third session of therapy, a medication evaluation would be scheduled. This agreement was documented.

Therapeutic Alliance

Developing a therapeutic alliance is a critical task in the first session. A strong alliance is known to increase treatment compliance, decrease the likelihood of early termination, and improve treatment outcomes (Horvath & Luborsky, 1993; Sperry, 2010a). Some therapists have come to interchange the terms "therapeutic alliance" and "therapeutic relationship." This is inaccurate as the therapeutic alliance is much greater than the relationship. Whereas the therapeutic relationship usually refers to the bond between client and therapist, the therapeutic alliance encompasses the bond, mutual agreement on treatment goals, and mutual agreement on treatment methods (Bordin, 1994). To form a bond with the therapist, the client should feel understood, comfortable, and hopeful about the course of therapy. In describing the four phases of the therapeutic process in Adlerian therapy, Dreikurs (1967) characterized the relationship as one of trust, encouragement, and mutual respect. This fosters courage so that the client not only can discuss sensitive topics, but also can shift to more adaptive ways of thinking, feeling, and behaving (Sperry & Carlson, 2014).

Identifying therapeutic goals and interventions requires the therapist to accurately identify the client's private logic and lifestyle convictions. The therapist must identify client expectations for treatment and the client's preferred approach. Some clients may voice their specific desires and hopes for therapy, while others may not. Structured questions can help the client and therapist identify and agree on goals. Additionally, some clients might prefer gaining insight through mutual exploration, while others prefer more concrete actions they can take to control their symptoms. Therapists adept at forming effective therapeutic alliances will collaboratively assess the client's needs.

Once the therapeutic alliance is established, it is essential that it be monitored and maintained to avoid strains or ruptures (i.e., tensions or breakdowns in the collaborative relationship). A rupture of the therapeutic alliance is considered a treatment-interfering factor that can negatively impact the outcome of treatment (Sperry, 2010b).

The therapist will administer the session rating scale (SRS) at the end of each session to evaluate and monitor the therapeutic alliance. For example, a client might feel disappointed that a topic was not covered during the session. In this case, a brief conversation about the rating and clarification of client needs and expectations and the therapist's awareness and opening of these needs and expectations in subsequent sessions. Such an understanding and agreement can enhance the therapeutic alliance where it might otherwise have become strained or ruptured.

Assessment

Assessment is focused on identifying possible diagnoses; the client's lifestyle and presenting problem; and precipitating, predisposing, and perpetuating factors. Accurate assessment aids the therapist in forming a case conceptualization, identifying therapeutic goals and interventions, and anticipating challenges. Assessment does not only provide information that the clinician can use to foster the therapeutic alliance; the process itself can build the alliance as the therapist conveys warmth, validation, and active listening. Clark (2002) finds that collection of early recollections during the assessment phase can also bolster the therapeutic alliance by helping clients feel safe discussing sensitive information.

The initial part of the session is comprised of a traditional diagnostic assessment. Assessment also includes identifying the client's pattern and level of social interest. This information is obtained through the diagnostic interview, early recollections, family constellation, and scores from various screening instruments.

Diagnostic Assessment

Like the intake evaluation in other therapeutic approaches, the first session of Adlerian pattern-focused therapy includes a traditional diagnostic assessment. The therapist asks specific questions that rule in possible diagnoses and rule out any comorbidity. To accomplish this and leave adequate time for the other first session tasks, the therapist must ask structured questions rather than more open-ended ones. When assessing client pattern, the therapist determines if the pattern is severe enough to warrant a personality disorder diagnosis. See the case example that follows for a demonstration of a full diagnostic assessment completed within about 15 minutes of the therapy session.

Lifestyle Assessment

Once the diagnostic assessment is complete, the therapist moves into assessing the client's lifestyle. This portion includes understanding how the client deals with life tasks of love, work, society, self, and spirituality, as well as eliciting the family constellation and early recollections and identifying the client's lifestyle syllogism.

Early Recollections

Eliciting early recollections in the first session helps the clinician build the therapeutic alliance and ascertain the client's lifestyle convictions and level of social interest.

Family Constellation

When assessing family constellation, the therapist obtains information about the client's relationships with family members, as well as the relationships between other family members.

Lifestyle Convictions

In Adlerian therapy, one's personal views about life are known as the lifestyle or style of life. The lifestyle is self-perpetuating and informs how a person perceives events, thoughts, feelings, and behaviors. Lifestyle convictions are essential in developing an Adlerian case conceptualization (Clark, 2002; Sperry & Sperry, 2012).

Pattern

A primary goal of this assessment is identifying the client's maladaptive pattern, which should then be mutually agreed on with the client. Gathering early recollections, lifestyle convictions, and family constellation information helps the therapist identify the maladaptive pattern. When assessing pattern, the therapist evaluates if the pattern is a personality style or is severe enough to merit a personality disorder diagnosis.

Social Interest

In the first session, the therapist determines level of social interest by analyzing early recollections, lifestyle, and pattern. The Social Interest Inventory-Short Form (SII-SF) is used to assist in the assessment of social interest and community feeling. The section below describes the SII-SF.

Use of Screeners

Screening instruments can also be useful in determining the client's diagnosis, as well as monitoring changes over time. These and other screeners have previously been described in chapter 3. The Patient Health Questionnaire-9 (PHQ-9) is useful in screening and monitoring level of depression, and the Social Interest Inventory-Short Form (SII-SF) is used to determine level of social interest.

The Patient Health Questionnaire-9 (PHQ-9) is a nine-item questionnaire corresponding to the nine DSM-5 criteria for major depressive disorder. Each question is rated on a four-point Likert-type scale from zero to three where 0 = not at all, 1 = several days, 2 = more than half the days, and 3 = nearly every day. A tenth question asks how any symptoms the client rated between 1 and 3 have interfered with the client's ability to function at work, at home, and with other people. Respondents rate their experiences for the previous two weeks. The scoring for the PHQ-9 is as follows: 0–4 = minimal or none, 5–9 = mild, 10–14 = moderate, 15–19 = moderately severe, 20–27 = severe. The client completes the PHQ-9 prior to each weekly session.

The Social Interest Index-Short Form (SII-SF) is an 11-item instrument used to measure levels of social interest. Each question is rated on a five-point Likert-type scale with a total range score of 11 to 55. Higher levels of social interest are indicated by higher SSI-SF scores (Leak, 2006). The client completes the SSI-SF before the first session, before the fifth session, and before the final session.

Socializing the Client to Treatment

The therapist introduces the client to the therapeutic approach, explaining its main purpose and focus as well as what is expected of the client. The therapist explains the protocol and allows the client to ask any questions. Finally, the therapist asks permission to determine if the client is willing to proceed in this therapeutic process. Doing so gives the client a sense of autonomy, builds credibility in the clinician and treatment approach, and increases client hopefulness.

Treatment Goals

The first session provides a setting for establishing first order, second order, and third order treatment goals with the client. Treatment goals should be achievable, realistic, and measurable. The client must agree on treatment goals, view them as attainable, and commit to working toward them.

First Order Goals

As described in chapter 3, first order goals are primarily shorter-term goals that include symptom reduction and the resolution of the presenting problem. Return to baseline (i.e., previous) level of functioning and improvement in daily functioning are important first order goals. In the case of Jennifer, the first order goals are to reduce her depressive symptoms, increase her activity and motivation, and increase social functioning.

Second Order Goals

Second order goals are longer-term goals of changing personality dynamics, which in this approach involves the client's maladaptive pattern. Specifically, it involves replacing or shifting from a maladaptive to a more adaptive pattern. An adaptive pattern is identified and agreed on by the therapist and client in the first session. The adaptive pattern is typically the opposite of the maladaptive pattern (Sperry & Carlson, 2014). For example, in the case of Jennifer, Jennifer's maladaptive pattern is being overly conscientious to the point of reduced effectiveness. Her adaptive pattern, then, is to be reasonably conscientious while still being effective. Accordingly, her second order goal is to shift to a more adaptive pattern of being reasonably conscientious while maintaining effectiveness.

Third Order Goals

Third order change refers to pattern change initiated and carried through by the client. In doing so, clients act as their own therapists by identifying and altering maladaptive responses. Third order change should be the ultimate therapeutic goal as it allows the client to effectively respond to life stressors in an adaptive way without the need for continuing therapy. The primary process in moving toward third order change is building client awareness. The more clients become aware of their own patterns, responses, and consequences, the more likely it is for them to effect third order change. The client must also take responsibility for his or her responses. Third order change is not likely to occur on its own. The therapist must begin helping clients gain awareness and encourage clients to effectively modify their responses (Sperry & Carlson, 2014). Typically, third order change goals are not addressed in the first session but occur as therapy proceeds. However, an essential part of the first session is preparing the client for post-therapy through increasing awareness and encouragement.

Effecting Initial Change

Adler stressed the collaborative, egalitarian relationship, and Dreikurs (1967) stressed that the therapist must ensure the client feels understood and must instill hope about the treatment (Kern, Stoltz, Gottlieb-Low, & Frost, 2009). Effecting some change within the first session helps build clinician credibility and instill hopefulness about the outcomes of therapy. Clients in distress are more likely to continue treatment if some change is effected in the first session (Sperry & Carlson, 2014). This can be achieved by helping reframe the client's problem, offering emotional first-aid, using a novel strategy such as a paradoxical suggestion or other very brief interventions.

Case of Jennifer

Diagnostic Impression

The case of Jennifer was introduced in chapter 3. Jennifer is a 21-year-old college student who meets criteria for Major Depressive Disorder (Moderate), Single Episode. She also displays an obsessive-compulsive personality style, missing the diagnosis of Obsessive-Compulsive Personality Disorder by one criteria. She was referred by her physician for therapy because she did not want medication for her depressive symptoms. Jennifer was administered the Patient Health Questionnaire-9 (PHQ-9), on which she scored a 13, indicating moderate depression. Her score on the Social Interest Inventory-Short Form (SSI-SF) was 21, indicating a low level of social interest. Jennifer's presenting symptoms have been interfering with her ability to focus on and complete her schoolwork effectively and have led to increased social isolation. These consequences only serve to decrease Jennifer's social interest and increase her depression. See Chapter 3 for a full summary of the case of Jennifer, including diagnosis and lifestyle assessment.

TABLE 4.2 Session 1 Assessment Scores

Patient Health Questionnaire-9 (PHQ-9)	13 (*moderate depression*)
Social Interest Inventory-Short Form (SSI-SF)	21
SRS	38
MI scores	Importance: 10 Confidence: 6

Transcription of Session 1

THERAPIST: Hi, Jennifer. It is nice to meet you. (smiles and shakes hands with client).

JENNIFER: Hi, it's nice to meet you as well.

THERAPIST: Today's session will be a little different from our future meetings. I will be asking you a number of questions today, so I can get a better understanding of what you have been experiencing and how you have been feeling. How does that sound?

Commentary

The therapist began the initial interaction with verbal and non-verbal communication intended to foster the rapport. By asking Jennifer permission to go on, the therapist helped build the therapeutic alliance. Asking permission created a more egalitarian relationship and allowed Jennifer to feel more in control of the session and treatment.

JENNIFER: That sounds fine. I don't mind answering some questions.

THERAPIST: Okay, good. To start off, can you tell me a little more about why you are seeking counseling?

JENNIFER: Well, I just haven't been feeling like myself lately. I have so much going on with school; it's been super stressful. I feel really overwhelmed and I've been really tired a lot. I actually missed a deadline for a project, which I never do. I was so upset, but I just felt too tired to complete everything on time.

THERAPIST: I am sorry to hear you have been feeling this way. You said you feel overwhelmed and tired. Can you tell me a little more about how your mood has been? **(Rule in/Rule out Major Depressive Disorder)**

JENNIFER: Um, my mood has actually been pretty low. I feel down a lot, or like I am just dragging.

THERAPIST: How often do you feel that way? **(R/I MDD)**

JENNIFER: Pretty much every day, most of the day. Sometimes I feel a little better but overall really low.

THERAPIST: What about things you used to enjoy? Do you still do those? **(R/I MDD)**

JENNIFER: Not that much anymore. I haven't been working out as often. I feel like I have no energy. I got so busy with school that I stopped hanging out with my friends as much, and now I don't even feel like doing it.

THERAPIST: So, it doesn't appeal to you the way it used to?

JENNIFER: Yes, that's right. I just haven't enjoyed anything lately. Everything just seems really blah. The last time I went out with my friends, I just wasn't into it. I just wanted to go home. I don't know if they noticed anything was wrong. We were all supposed to go to this event on campus that week and I just didn't go.

THERAPIST: Okay, you mentioned you feel tired often. Can you tell me more about that? **(R/I MDD)**

JENNIFER: Yes, I feel tired almost all the time, it seems like. Even if I get a day where I can sleep in, I still feel tired all day. It's also really hard to focus on everything I have to do. I feel foggy. Like it's hard to focus on my work. That's why I've been putting a lot of things off.

THERAPIST: Okay, so you feel tired a lot and you also have had a difficult time concentrating. **(R/I MDD)**

JENNIFER: Right.

THERAPIST: Can you tell me how your sleep has been? **(R/I MDD)**

JENNIFER: I oversleep a lot lately. It seems like I'm always tired when I wake up and I end up going back to sleep when I should be getting up. A couple of days ago, I accidentally slept through my alarm and when I woke up it was 11:00 a.m. I don't know how that happened. And what was crazy was that I was still tired, even after I got all that sleep.

THERAPIST: It must be difficult for you to feel tired so often when you have so much on your plate.

JENNIFER: Yes, it is.

THERAPIST: How long would you say you have been feeling this way? **(R/I MDD; R/O Persistent Depressive Disorder).**

JENNIFER: Probably about three weeks. It feels like longer but it's been about three weeks.

THERAPIST: Have you ever experienced any similar feelings before? **(R/I MDD; R/O recurrent episode)**

JENNIFER: No, I haven't. This is the first time I have felt this way.

THERAPIST: Have you ever been to a therapist or psychiatrist or sought treatment before?

JENNIFER: No, I haven't.

THERAPIST: Has any doctor ever prescribed you any psychiatric medications before?

JENNIFER: No, I have never been given any medications. I've never been prescribed anything or taken anything.

THERAPIST: Okay. How would you say these symptoms have been affecting your everyday life?

JENNIFER: Well, I don't do anything I like anymore. Like I said, I haven't seen my friends and I've missed some study groups, which are very important and something I used to actually enjoy. I'm mostly worried about my grades. I am a pre-law major so I am taking required and difficult courses right now. These are things law schools weigh heavily. I just feel so much pressure, like if I mess up now, I won't be able to follow through with my career the way I want to. It's really upsetting. I haven't even told my parents because grades are so important to them. I don't want them to think I'm not doing well in my classes.

THERAPIST: I understand. You have been isolating from your friends and parents and missing some important activities. And you have had difficulty keeping up with your schoolwork, which worries you because your career is very important to you.

JENNIFER: Yes, that's right. I feel guilty about how much I have been slacking off. I mean, I am still actually keeping my grades up, but I know I could be doing more. I could be doing better. I feel really bad about it and think about that all the time.

THERAPIST: Okay, so you have had feelings of guilt, in addition, even though you still perform well in school? **(R/I MDD)**

JENNIFER: Yes, definitely.

THERAPIST: I understand that this has been a difficult experience for you. I appreciate your cooperation answering these questions. I have several more if that is okay.

JENNIFER: Yes, that's fine.

THERAPIST: Thank you. You told me about things that have changed for you recently, like your sleep patterns and your energy level. Has your weight changed recently?

JENNIFER: No, it's been about the same.

THERAPIST: So, no weight gain or weight loss recently?

JENNIFER: No.

THERAPIST: Have you ever felt like you had extra energy, where you perhaps didn't need to sleep as much? **(R/O Bipolar Disorder)**

JENNIFER: Not really. I definitely had more energy before, but I never felt like a surge of energy or anything like that. I could go without sleep, but not for long. I would be very tired if I missed my sleep.

THERAPIST: Do you ever have mood swings, sometimes up and sometimes down? **(R/O Bipolar)**

JENNIFER: No, I wouldn't say I've ever had mood swings. Things get on my nerves sometimes but I'm never really up and down. Like happy, then sad, or anything like that.

THERAPIST: Okay. Have you had any major changes in your life recently? **(R/O Adjustment Disorder)**

JENNIFER: No, not really. I've been here at school for over a year. Nothing big has really happened since then.

THERAPIST: What about any event that made you feel really frightened or out of control? **(R/O Post Traumatic Stress Disorder)**

JENNIFER: No, I haven't experienced anything like that.

THERAPIST: Okay, would you also describe yourself as a nervous person? **(screen for anxiety disorders).**

JENNIFER: Um, I get worried about missing my schoolwork and deadlines. But I wouldn't label myself a nervous person.

THERAPIST: So, you worry about your schoolwork. Is there anything else that you worry about?

JENNIFER: Um, not really. No.

THERAPIST: You mentioned you have withdrawn somewhat from social situations. Have you ever had difficulty in social situations, maybe fear of giving a presentation or something like that? **(R/O Social Anxiety Disorder)**

JENNIFER: No, I actually like giving presentations. I've started going out less with my friends mostly because I was so busy and too stressed and recently because I have just felt too tired and like I don't really care.

THERAPIST: Okay, I understand. Are there any places you are afraid to go to or things you are afraid to do? **(R/O Agoraphobia)**

JENNIFER: No, I don't experience anything like that.

THERAPIST: Do you have any specific fears that are especially worrisome to you, such as flying or heights or anything like that? **(R/O specific phobia)**

JENNIFER: No, I don't have any fears specifically like that. I don't like bugs or spiders, but I'm not like deathly afraid of them.

THERAPIST: Okay, have you ever felt fear so intense that you thought you might die, have a heart attack, or stop breathing? **(R/O Panic Disorder)**

JENNIFER: No, I can't say I have ever experienced something like that.

Commentary

The therapist continued the diagnostic evaluation to rule in DSM-5 Major Depressive Disorder and rule out anxiety and stress-related disorders (American Psychiatric Association, 2013). During the interview process, the therapist displayed a warm demeanor and practiced active listening and reflecting in order to build rapport and facilitate the therapeutic alliance. Jennifer revealed she has been isolating herself and skipping social events and study groups. This points to her decreased social interest, which will be an area of focus during treatment.

THERAPIST: Okay, do you ever have recurring thoughts that bad things will happen or are there any repetitive or ritualistic behaviors you feel compelled to do? **(R/O Obsessive-Compulsive Disorder)**

JENNIFER: No, I like being organized. Sometimes people have complained that I stick to my routines too much. Lately, I haven't been as much. But I don't have any rituals or repetitive behaviors like that.

THERAPIST: When you say you have routines, and that people have complained, do you find it difficult to stray from those routines even if something else comes up?

JENNIFER: It's difficult, but I can. Like if I planned to organize my work, I could go out with my friends instead and then organize later. But it can be difficult.

THERAPIST: So, you can be flexible but with some difficulty sometimes? **(R/I obsessive-compulsive personality style; R/O Obsessive-Compulsive Personality Disorder)**

JENNIFER: Yes, that pretty much describes it.

THERAPIST: Okay, just a few more questions. Have you ever had any strange or unusual experiences? **(screen for psychotic disorder)**

JENNIFER: No, I can't think of anything unusual.

THERAPIST: Okay, have you ever heard voices, believed that people meant to harm you, or lost touch with reality? **(R/O psychotic disorder)**

JENNIFER: No, I haven't.

THERAPIST: Would people ever say you have strange ideas? **(screen for delusional disorder)**

JENNIFER: Um, no nobody has ever said that.

THERAPIST: Do you ever feel like your mind plays tricks on you? (**screen for dissociative disorder)**

JENNIFER: I don't think so. Like what?

THERAPIST: Like feeling detached from reality, outside of your own body, or having periods in your life you can't remember. **(screen for dissociative disorder)**

JENNIFER: No, definitely not. That sounds very scary.

THERAPIST: How has your memory been serving you lately? **(screen for neurocognitive disorder)**

JENNIFER: Um, my memory is okay. It has been hard to concentrate, like I said. Hard to focus. But I don't think my memory has been bad.

THERAPIST: So, no recent decline in your memory?

JENNIFER: No, no decline.

THERAPIST: Now, I know you said you haven't lost or gained any weight recently, but has food or eating ever been a problem for you? **(screen for eating disorders)**

JENNIFER: No, it hasn't. I eat healthy but not too strict. I wouldn't say I ever overeat or anything like that.

THERAPIST: Have you ever eaten a very large amount of food in one sitting, where you felt you could not control how much you were eating? **(R/O binge eating)**

JENNIFER: No, I have never done that.

THERAPIST: Have you ever restricted the amount of food you eat? **(R/O anorexia)**

JENNIFER: No, I haven't.

THERAPIST: Have you ever felt you had to compensate for food you ate, by throwing up, taking laxatives, or exercising excessively? **(R/O bulimia)**

JENNIFER: No way, I have never done or wanted to do anything like that.

THERAPIST: Okay, and can you tell me about your drug and alcohol use? **(screen for Substance Use Disorder)**

JENNIFER: I really don't use much alcohol. I drink only occasionally when I am out with my friends. It doesn't have that much appeal to me. I don't like to feel drunk. I don't use any drugs either. I never have. It's popular for people to take drugs to study, like ADHD drugs. People have offered them to me but even though I'm really concerned about my work, I just feel too freaked out to take anything. It's just not for me.

THERAPIST: Okay, so there isn't a possibility that a substance has anything to do with how you have been feeling recently?

JENNIFER: No.

THERAPIST: What about any prescription or over-the-counter medications? **(screen for Medication-Induced Substance Disorder)**

JENNIFER: I don't have any prescriptions. I take something for a headache sometimes, and I take allergy medicine sometimes. It's the non-drowsy kind, though. That's really it.

THERAPIST: Do you have any medical conditions? **(screen for medical conditions)**

JENNIFER: No, I'm healthy. I just had a physical about three months ago when I was home for summer break. They said everything looked good.

THERAPIST: Okay, that is good. Now, since you have been dealing with this low mood, have you had any thoughts of harming yourself or felt that life wasn't worth living? **(R/O suicidal ideation)**

JENNIFER: No, definitely not. I haven't had any ideas like that.

THERAPIST: Okay, what about any thoughts about hurting someone else? **(R/O homicidal ideation)**

JENNIFER: No, definitely not that either. No way.

THERAPIST: How would you describe yourself as a person, Jennifer? **(screen for personality disorders)**

JENNIFER: Um, I don't know. I guess I would say I'm a pretty focused person. I usually like to stay organized and focus on my school and my extra-curricular stuff. I like to stay active and play sports. I play softball.

THERAPIST: Okay, you mentioned that people have complained that you like your routines too much. Is that a common thing for you? **(R/I obsessive-compulsive personality style)**

JENNIFER: Um, I guess so. My friends tease me sometimes. Like they will want to go out but it's my day to clean my apartment. And they will say, "Oh you're so lame!" Or something like that. But I can reschedule certain things or be somewhat flexible if I need to.

THERAPIST: Do you ever find yourself so focused on organizing, making lists, or paying attention to details that you lose sight of what you were originally trying to do? **(R/I obsessive compulsive personality style)**

JENNIFER: Oh, yes. Wow, that sure sounds like me. I remember my first year of college; I got so focused on some small details of an assignment that I did the assignment incorrectly. I ended up getting a B minus. I was freaking out over it! I ended up doing way more work than I needed to do but, in the end, I missed the main point of the assignment, which was actually pretty easy and simple.

THERAPIST: Okay, so you overcomplicated the assignment by focusing on some minor details to the point where you completed the assignment incorrectly?

JENNIFER: Yes.

THERAPIST: So, sometimes you can get in your own way by being so overly conscientious, maybe even a little perfectionistic, that it interferes with the things you must do? **(identify pattern: being overly conscientious to the point of reduced effectiveness)**

JENNIFER: (Pause) I mean, I don't like to admit that, but yes that happens. It's actually very useful for me to be organized. I find it annoying when other people do things sloppily. It just seems like a lot of people don't think about the details enough. Maybe I sometimes think about the details a little too much, though. Some people have said I'm a perfectionist before. I guess I would agree with that.

THERAPIST: Right. Being organized and paying attention to details can be very useful traits. I am sure they have helped contribute to your academic success. It may be even more helpful to you if you can find a balance between being conscientious and perfectionistic while still being effective in the ways you want to be. **(second order goal)**

JENNIFER: Yes, I would agree with that. It can be so frustrating. And then I think, "Oh, why did I do that? What's wrong with me?" You know? I should have just gotten organized and done my work instead of getting super focused on something small and going off on a tangent.

THERAPIST: Right. It would probably save you a lot of time that would be useful to you as well.

JENNIFER: That's true. I would like to be more efficient.

THERAPIST: Would you say it is also a pattern for you to avoid social interactions or fun activities because you are so focused on your work? **(R/O R/I Obsessive-Compulsive Personality Disorder)**

JENNIFER: I started doing that when I got really overwhelmed, but for the most part I wouldn't say that's really a problem for me. Usually I can fit in fun activities or time with people I care about.

THERAPIST: That is good. Do you ever find it difficult to throw out old objects, even if they are worn out or have no value anymore? **(R/O OCPD)**

JENNIFER: No, I like to clean up and throw out junk.

THERAPIST: Okay, you said you feel frustrated with others sometimes, because they are not as organized as you. Have you found it difficult to work with others or delegate tasks because people won't do things the way you like them done? **(R/O OCPD)**

JENNIFER: Um, it's difficult. People have accused me of nitpicking, but I can work with others. I like working in groups, especially if I can get paired up with a friend. Sometimes I struggle with that, but I can generally manage it.

THERAPIST: How are you with handling money? Would you consider yourself a spender or a saver? **(R/O OCPD)**

JENNIFER: Well, I don't have much money right now, but my parents help me. I like to save and plan, but I also enjoy shopping and going out. Spending money on a girls' day, movies, ice cream, things like that.

THERAPIST: Okay, so you find that you can balance staying on budget and treating yourself once in a while?

JENNIFER: Yes, I can.

Commentary

Several other DSM-5 diagnoses have also been screened and ruled out. Jennifer's responses indicate obsessive-compulsive personality style. Earlier in this evaluation, the diagnosis of Major Depressive Disorder was made. Her maladaptive pattern is being overly conscientious and perfectionistic to the point of reduced effectiveness. The therapist ruled out obsessive-compulsive personality disorder, as Jennifer does not meet full criteria. Jennifer's pattern serves to decrease her social interest and increase her sense of discouragement. The rigid rules Jennifer imposes on herself, coupled with her self-criticism, reduce her ability to adequately engage with others, thus exacerbating her depression. Jennifer's private logic is that she must execute all things perfectly to be worthy of others.

THERAPIST: Please tell me a little more about what your family is like. What was it like growing up in your home? **(family constellation)**

JENNIFER: Well, I'm the oldest. I have a younger sister and a little brother. My sister is four years younger than me and my brother is two years younger. I would say my childhood was okay. My parents always made sure we had what we needed, especially stuff for school and extra-curriculars. Like the violin lessons. And I remember having a tutor and being involved in numerous sports. But there was also a lot of pressure on me. My parents expect a lot from me. They expected me to always keep my grades up and work hard. **(birth order)**

THERAPIST: Okay, so your parents gave you a lot of opportunities that you appreciated but they also put a lot of pressure on you to succeed.

JENNIFER: That's right.

THERAPIST: What was it like being the oldest child in your family?

JENNIFER: Oh, well again my parents put a lot of pressure on me to succeed. And they would say I had to be a role model to my brother and sister. I never had a close relationship with either one of my siblings. It just always felt like we were all doing our own thing. We got on each other's nerves a lot. Just having to share a bathroom or my sister would take my clothes or makeup without asking. They could be very annoying. I remember one time when I was a freshman in high school; I had a really long day and came home late after softball practice and I still needed to do some homework before going to bed. Then I saw that my brother and sister had put Post-it notes all over my desk and all my stuff as a prank. Then I was the one who had to clean it up. Just annoying stuff like that. And I couldn't get mad at them or then my parents would be upset with me. My relationship with my little sister is weird.

THERAPIST: Can you tell me more about that?

JENNIFER: Well, sometimes I envy what she has. She is so laid back. She seems to not have a care in the world. Like she just hangs out with her friends and has a good time. She's like, "Oh, the universe will give you what you need, so just relax." Which is super annoying because she's completely clueless. But sometimes, I think I wish I could be that clueless. Things would probably be easier!

THERAPIST: Can you describe your relationship with your parents for me a little more?

JENNIFER: Um, my relationship with them is fine. They can be a little critical of me, but they really care and they always want what's best for me.

THERAPIST: Which parent were you most like?

JENNIFER: Probably more like my dad. He's also athletic and hard-working.

THERAPIST: Who was your mother's favorite among your siblings?

JENNIFER: Oh, my sister for sure. They are more alike. My sister could get away with anything.

THERAPIST: Who was your father's favorite?

JENNIFER: I don't know. I guess I would have to say me. Because even though my brother is the only boy, he's not that athletic. My father and I have that in common.

THERAPIST: Please describe the relationship between your parents.

JENNIFER: My parents get along. I think their relationship is pretty good.

THERAPIST: Okay, who would you say made the big decisions?

JENNIFER: My parents sort of share those responsibilities. My dad is the breadwinner, primarily. My mom has worked just part time for a while, and before that she stayed home for a few years.

THERAPIST: How did they solve problems and deal with conflicts?

JENNIFER: Um, they would argue sometimes. They seemed to work a lot of things out but there were some things they seemed to never work out. My mom would complain that my dad worked too much. And my dad gets really annoyed when my mom is late to things or when she takes too long to get ready. He says she has poor time-management skills.

THERAPIST: Do you remember your parents ever working out a specific conflict?

JENNIFER: Not really working it out. They mostly would just avoid talking about things. Like they might get upset for a little bit but then they would just avoid it and act like nothing happened.

THERAPIST: Okay, so they mostly avoided talking about and resolving conflicts. Did your parents show affection openly?

JENNIFER: Not really. My mom would kiss my dad goodbye every morning before he left for work and hello every evening when he got home but that's it. I never saw them cuddle or say loving things to each other.

THERAPIST: Okay, which parent was primarily in charge of discipline?

JENNIFER: Um, I guess my dad. My mom would pretty much agree with whatever my dad said. If we ever thought something was unfair, she would just say, "You need to listen to your father," or something like that.

THERAPIST: Who did you go to when you were hurt or frightened?

JENNIFER: Probably my mom. She is always there for me. Especially when I was younger and really needed a lot more from her. She stayed home and was really invested in our lives. She still is. She drove us everywhere and participated in all our activities. She always volunteered for stuff at school and on my athletic teams.

THERAPIST: Okay, so you feel like your mom has been there to support you?

JENNIFER: Yes, she always has been. I mean sometimes she doesn't get it. She doesn't always understand what I'm dealing with, and I don't always want to tell her everything. But for the most part I know she is there for me.

THERAPIST: What were some of your family values growing up?

JENNIFER: My parents really valued achievement and success, like I said before. They really value hard work and success. They always told us that was the most important thing, to go to college and get a good job.

THERAPIST: What were you expected to be or do when you grew up?

JENNIFER: Oh, it was expected that I would go into law, business, or medicine. My parents flat out said that too me. They would always tell me that people who majored in liberal arts or humanities didn't make any money or couldn't get jobs. That's okay because I was pretty sure I wanted to do law when I was in high school. I was on the debate team. That's something I really enjoyed.

Commentary

The therapist used more closed-ended questions to assess Jennifer's family constellation. While reflective statements from the therapist were not as evident in this exchange, the therapist displayed a warm and nonjudgmental stance, leading Jennifer to feel more comfortable disclosing information and building the bond between Jennifer and the therapist. Jennifer's family constellation reveals key information about the origin of her lifestyle and perfectionistic pattern. See chapter 3 for an interpretation of Jennifer's family constellation and lifestyle.

THERAPIST: Now, Jennifer, can you tell me one of your earliest recollections? Think back to when you were younger, before age eight, and tell me the first thing you can remember. It should be a single experience that you can recall, rather than something someone told you happened. **(early recollections)**

JENNIFER: Um, well when I was six, I was really into building things. My parents had bought me this very cool set of toy bricks. I spent a lot of time with them. So, one time I spent like a week building this elaborate structure. I worked so hard on it. I must have spent several hours a day every day just intensely focused on this thing and I was just so into it. So, one day I come home from school and I saw that my younger sister had knocked it over! It was ridiculous! I usually kept my bedroom door closed but I guess my mom had been cleaning and left it open or something. I don't know. But my sister had gotten in there and destroyed it. **(early recollections 1)**

THERAPIST: Okay, so you spent all this time, every day for a week, working on an elaborate structure out of toy bricks only to find that your sister had knocked it down and broken it while you were at school. Is that right?

JENNIFER: Yes, that's correct. And then I was so mad I pushed my sister. Of course, she fell on her butt and started crying. Then my parents punished me by taking away my after-dinner TV time.

THERAPIST: Okay, so you pushed her down and then you were punished.

JENNIFER: Yes.

THERAPIST: So, what is the most vivid part of that recollection: If the whole scene was on videotape, where would you push the pause button?

JENNIFER: Just seeing the tower I built in pieces all over the floor. I remember walking in and not seeing the tower, then seeing the pieces all over the floor and slowly realizing what had happened.

THERAPIST: What were you thinking at that moment?

JENNIFER: I thought, "It's ruined! All my hard work." You know? "My sister makes trouble for me and then I'm the one who gets punished. It's not fair."

THERAPIST: Okay, so you thought it was not fair. It was ruined. How did you feel?

JENNIFER: I felt angry, but I didn't show it. I mean, I pushed my sister, but I tried holding my feelings inside. I didn't yell or show it on my face.

THERAPIST: Okay, can you think of another early memory, also before age eight, that you can recall from being there?

JENNIFER: Uh, yes. When I was eight years old. I used to play violin. My parents got me lessons and I played at school where we had recitals. So, I had a violin recital at school and I made two small mistakes during my part. Then afterwards, when my parents were driving me home, they yelled at me for making those mistakes. They said I wasn't practicing enough and they were spending all this money on lessons. **(ER 2)**

THERAPIST: Ok, so you had a violin recital at school and you made two small mistakes while you were playing and then your parents yelled at you for not practicing enough. Is that right?

JENNIFER: Yes. That's what I remember happening.

THERAPIST: What do you remember the most about that? What was the most vivid part of your memory?

JENNIFER: Just making those mistakes. I can still see myself making them. One was a slightly wrong chord and the other was my finger slipped off the bow and I sort of dragged it across the strings and it made a weird sound.

THERAPIST: What were you thinking at that moment?

JENNIFER: Ugh, that I worked so hard and I failed. I thought, "I failed, I can't stand it!"

THERAPIST: Okay, "I worked so hard and failed. I can't stand it." How did you feel?

JENNIFER: I felt embarrassed and sad. I felt worried, too. About how everything would turn out.

THERAPIST: Okay, so you felt embarrassed, sad, and worried.

JENNIFER: Yes.

THERAPIST: That's very good. Thank you for answering my questions. You have helped me get a better understanding of the symptoms you are experiencing and how they have been affecting your daily life, as well as a better idea of what it was like for you growing up and your career goals. Before we wrap up, I would like to formalize the informed consent agreement, as well as learn what you hope to achieve in our work together over the next several weeks.

[Then, informed consent was discussed. It was noted that consent is more than an event (i.e., signing the consent form, but also as a process that would continue throughout remaining sessions if any changes in treatment focus arose. This also included "permission seeking," a form of consent.]

Commentary

Jennifer was quite cooperative with the elicitation of early recollections, as she was when discussing her family constellation. The therapist reflected, restated, and validated Jennifer's account of her experiences and emotions. The therapist then thanked Jennifer for sharing and explained how Jennifer's responses were helpful to the therapist and the therapeutic process, before asking permission to proceed to treatment goals. This exchange further enhanced the developing therapeutic alliance, built clinician credibility, and served to not trigger Jennifer's maladaptive pattern while discussing sensitive topics. Treatment goals were set, and informed consent was discussed, including provision for when and if medication would be combined with therapy. Then, the was document signed.

JENNIFER: I would like to have a better mood, sort of shake off this tired and dragging feeling. I'd like to be more motivated to do my work or to do some of my hobbies and things I enjoy again.

THERAPIST: Okay, so you would like to address your low mood and decrease your sadness as well as increase your energy level. You would also like to increase your motivation as well as your enjoyment of activities such as socializing and pursuing your hobbies. Is that correct? **(first order change goals)**

JENNIFER: Yes, I would really like to do that. Hopefully that's something that's possible. It worries me that I'll continue to feel this way. I really hope counseling can do it because I don't want to take medication unless it is necessary.

THERAPIST: I hear your concern about medication. And, yes, there is a very high likelihood that working together we can achieve these goals in therapy.

JENNIFER: Oh, that's good to hear.

THERAPIST: Earlier, we discussed you having a pattern of being perfectionistic and focusing on details to the point where it sometimes interferes with your work and your effectiveness. Is that something you would like to address? **(second order change goal)**

JENNIFER: (Pause) Yes, I really do. I like to stay organized and I think attention to details is a good thing. Especially in law. You must pay attention to small things. But sometimes I get really frustrated and get in my own way.

THERAPIST: Right. I think these are good goals and are reasonably achievable. We can spend the next few weeks working to help you achieve them and start feeling better and getting more of what you want. How does that sound?

JENNIFER: That sounds good. I feel a little better knowing that I have a plan now. **(agreement on treatment goals)**

Commentary

The therapist helped Jennifer identify both first and second order change goals, which were then mutually agreed upon. Jennifer was likely able to agree on her maladaptive pattern and desire to move toward a more adaptive one because she felt safe, understood, and validated through the assessment process. In discussing treatment goals, the clinician was able to join with Jennifer, instill hope in treatment, and build clinician credibility by effecting this change.

THERAPIST: Good. I am glad to hear that, and I look forward to working with you. Before we end, can you tell me on a scale from 0 to 10, with 0 being not at all and 10 being the most, how important is it for you to achieve the goals we outlined? **(motivational interviewing question #1]**

JENNIFER: I would say a 10. I really hate feeling this way and I want to feel like my old self again.

THERAPIST: So, it is very important. That's good. Now on the same scale, how confident are you that you can achieve these goals? **(MI question #2)**

JENNIFER: Um, I would say maybe 6. I'm not sure how it's going to happen. It's sort of hard to visualize.

THERAPIST: So, a 6 is more than halfway there. That's good. Before we end today I would like to give you some homework to work on until our next session. How does that sound?

JENNIFER: That sounds fine.

THERAPIST: What I'm going to give you is this daily mood rating sheet. It is broken up into two-hour intervals on the left column. You will write the dates of the week across the top. I want you to pay closer attention to your moods this week and write how you feel on the chart, every two hours. You can write one word or several. How does that sound?

JENNIFER: I can do that. Thanks.

THERAPIST: Next, please fill out this form called the Session Review Scale. It asks you to rate four items about how our session went today, and specifically if you got what you came for. Are you okay with that? **(SRS review)**

JENNIFER: Yes, certainly. That sounds interesting. (pause while she fills out form).

THERAPIST: (after reviewing the SRS and scoring it as 38 out of 40). It looks like you were satisfied with our session today and that we covered what you wanted to talk about.

JENNIFER: Yes, we did. (pause). I was hoping that I wouldn't be too nervous and that it would be easy to talk to you. My nerves went away quickly, and you made it easy for me to feel comfortable and hopeful. Thanks.

THERAPIST: I am so glad to hear that. (pause). I thought we worked together pretty well! And, I look forward to our future sessions together.

THERAPIST: Do you have any questions for me before we stop?

JENNIFER: No, not really.

THERAPIST: Okay, then I look forward to meeting with you next week.

JENNIFER: Me too.

Commentary

Jennifer's response to the confidence rating was higher than might be expected in an initial session, given her current presentation of depression. These responses presumably reflect her increased hope and trust in the therapist and the therapy process. In addition, her relatively high scores on the SRS suggest her approval of their therapeutic alliance in terms of bond, goals, and methods. Accordingly, there was no need for the therapist to utilize a very brief intervention to effect a change in the session, since it is most likely she will return for the next session.

Finally, it is noteworthy that the therapist did not inadvertently (or intentionally) trigger her maladaptive pattern in this session. This might have occurred had the therapist made a statement or comment that was perceived by the client as critical or demanding, resulting in a strain or rupture to the therapeutic alliance. Unless the therapist endeavors to repair the therapeutic alliance, it is unlikely the client would feel sufficiently confident and safe to return for the next session (Sperry, 2010a).

Concluding Note

The first session is crucial for building rapport and establishing the therapeutic alliance. To achieve this, the therapist is expected to display an open, nonjudgmental stance to approach the client and uses the diagnostic interview and collection of early recollections as opportunities to build the therapeutic alliance. The second key task in the first session is assessment. The therapist completes a diagnostic assessment and evaluates the client's level of social interest. Screeners can be used to provide information about the client's presenting problem as well as social interest. The therapist elicits the family constellation and early recollections and ascertains the client's pattern and lifestyle. Finally, both first and second order goals are specified and mutually agreed upon.

References

Bordin, E. S. (1994). Theory and research on the therapeutic working alliance: New directions. In A. O. Horvath & L. S. Greenberg (Eds.), *The working alliance: Theory, research, and practice* (pp. 13–37). New York, NY: John Wiley & Sons.

Clark, A. J. (2002). *Early recollections: Theory and practice in counseling and psychotherapy.* New York, NY: Brunner-Routledge.

Dreikurs, R. (1967). *Psychodynamics, psychotherapy, and counseling: The collected papers of Rudolf Dreikurs, M.D.* Chicago, IL: Alfred Adler Institute.

Horvath, A. O., & Luborsky, L. (1993). The role of the therapeutic alliance in psychotherapy. *Journal of Consulting and Clinical Psychology, 61*(4), 561–573.

Kern, R. M., Stoltz, K. B., Gottlieb-Low, H. B., & Frost, L. S. (2009). The therapeutic alliance and early recollections. *The Journal of Individual Psychology, 65*(2), 110–122.

Leak, G. K. (2006). Development and validation of a revised measure of Adlerian social interest. *Social Behavior & Personality: An International Journal, 34*, 443–449.

Manaster, G., & Corsini, R. (1982). *Individual psychology: Theory and practice.* Itasca, IL: F. E. Peacock.

Sperry, L. (2010a). *Highly effective therapy: Developing essential clinical competencies in counseling and psychotherapy.* New York, NY: Routledge.

Sperry, L. (2010b). *Core competencies in counseling and psychotherapy: Becoming a highly competent and effective therapist.* New York, NY: Routledge.

Sperry, L., Brill, P., Howard, K., & Grissom, G. (1996). *Treatment outcomes in psychotherapy and psychiatric interventions.* New York, NY: Brunner/Mazel.

Sperry, L., & Carlson, J. (2014). *How master therapists work: Effecting change from the first through the last session and beyond.* New York, NY: Routledge.

Sperry, L., & Sperry, J. (2012). *Case conceptualization. Mastering this competency with ease and confidence.* New York, NY: Routledge. Sperry, J., & Sperry, L. (2018). *Cognitive behavior therapy in professional counseling practice.* New York, NY: Routledge.

5

Session Two

Learning Objectives

In this chapter, you will learn the following:

1. How to implement the APFT query sequence
2. How to focus sessions to facilitate pattern change
3. How to use the acting "as if" intervention
4. How to conduct ongoing assessment
5. The continuing case of how Adlerian pattern-focused therapy is practiced

The second session begins with a review of the client's homework assignment of keeping a daily mood log. The Mood Scale score is then elicited, and the Outcome Rating Scale is reviewed. The core therapeutic strategy, the Adlerian pattern-focused query sequence is introduced and tailored to the client's responses on the assessment instruments. A variation of key Adlerian technique, acting "as if," called behavioral activation, is also introduced. The therapist continues to focus on building the therapeutic alliance in the session and measures the strength of the alliance using the Session Rating Scale. Homework is discussed and mutually agreed on. This chapter provides a description of these therapeutic techniques and illustrates them in a session transcription that includes commentary.

Query Sequence

The query sequence in Adlerian pattern-focused therapy consists of therapeutically processing nine queries, followed by a set of motivational interviewing questions. As noted in chapter 3, this sequence was derived from eight questions of Cognitive Behavior Analysis System of Psychotherapy (CBASP) (McCullough, 2000) and refashioned as nine queries (Sperry, 2005).

The query sequence focuses on identifying a client's thoughts and behaviors in a specific situation and analyzing whether those thoughts and behaviors were hurtful or helpful to the client achieving his or her desired outcome in the situation. Thoughts and behaviors identified as hurtful are then replaced with ones that would be more helpful in achieving the desired outcome. The situation elicited for process with the query sequence must be representative of the maladaptive pattern, and the intervention is introduced in terms of the pattern. Alternative thoughts and behaviors, reflective of the adaptive pattern, are generated to replace hurtful ones.

The client is asked to think of a recent situation in which the outcome was unsatisfactory to the client. The client's thoughts and behaviors during the situation are then elicited. The client is asked what his or her desired outcome was in this situation as well as what the actual outcome was. The therapist helps the client identify a desired outcome within his or her control. If the client did not achieve the desired outcome, the therapist asks permission to re-evaluate the situation with the client, in terms of the more adaptive pattern, and see how the outcome might have been different. Each thought and behavior is then processed in terms of how helpful or hurtful it was in achieving the desired outcome. The therapist asks how each thought or behavior was helpful or hurtful, and hurtful thoughts and behaviors are processed and replaced with more helpful ones. See chapter 3 for the full query sequence steps.

Replacement

The query sequence uses cognitive replacement, whereby thoughts and behaviors that reflect a client's maladaptive pattern are replaced with more adaptive ones (Sperry, 2018). As the counselor collaborates with the client to replace unhelpful thoughts and behaviors, the client learns to examine situations in a way that is more consequential. The client learns that attainment of one's goals can be affected by his or her thoughts, behaviors, and emotional responses. This strategy is founded in the Adlerian notion that people can become discouraged as they continuously fail to achieve their goals by approaching them from a maladaptive lifestyle. In this approach, the replacement strategy focuses on shifting the client's pattern from maladaptive to adaptive.

Pattern Shifting

As previously stated, the query sequence focuses on pattern change, constituting second order change. Because the core therapeutic strategy focuses on analyzing pattern-laden situations and generating alternative thoughts and behaviors that are reflective of an adaptive pattern, the client shifts from a maladaptive pattern to a more adaptive one. Changes in the client's lifestyle and an increase in social interest mark this shift. In the case of Jennifer, Jennifer's pattern of being perfectionistic to the point of reduced effectiveness will be reflected in her thoughts and behaviors in specific situations. Nearly always, the elicited situation reflects her maladaptive pattern, and the therapist helps her generate new thoughts and behaviors to reflect her adaptive pattern of being reasonably conscientious while maintaining effectiveness.

Acting "As If" and Behavioral Activation

The acting "as if" technique (Carlson, Watts, & Maniacci, 2006) instructs clients to behave as they would if the changes they desire had already been made. The client replaces less helpful behaviors with more helpful and healthy ones. A variant of the acting "as if" is behavioral activation. Essentially, behavioral activation engages an individual in pleasant and useful behaviors and activities as a replacement for inactive, avoidant, or unpleasant behaviors and activities.

To implement the behavioral activation intervention, the therapist first explains the rationale of the intervention. Then, the therapist helps the client generate a list of pleasurable activities and a list of necessary activities. The client is then asked to schedule at least one pleasurable activity and one necessary activity to complete in the following week. Fewer activities are scheduled at the beginning of treatment. To begin, activities should be easy to complete within 15 minutes, with backup activities identified, increasing the likelihood that activities will be completed. As treatment progresses, the number and duration of activities increases. Activities are scheduled on specific days and the therapist instructs the client to keep a log of activities and rate each one on a scale from 0–10 for both level of completion and level of enjoyment.

Ongoing Assessment

After completing the initial assessment in the first session, the focus turns to ongoing assessment to monitor symptom improvement, pattern change, increased social interest, and the strength of the therapeutic relationship. Progress monitoring has become increasingly important in psychotherapy and counseling as managed care companies hold therapists accountable for the success of their treatments (Meier, 2015). Additionally, it is estimated that treatment fails in up to 50% of cases (Persons & Mikami, 2002). Unfortunately, many therapists tend to overestimate the success of treatment (Hatfield, McCullough, Frantz, & Kreiger, 2010).

Therapeutic interventions that employ progress monitoring and ongoing assessment, and incorporate resulting information into treatment decisions, have been shown to increase the rate of client success (Meier, 2015). APFT uses the Outcome Rating Scale (ORS), the Mood Scale (MS), the Social Interest Index-Short Form (SSI-SF), and the Session Rating Scale (SRS) as progress monitoring measures. In the case example for the case of Jennifer, the Patient Health Questionnaire-9 (PHQ-9) is used to monitor Jennifer's symptoms of depression. The PHQ-9 and SSI-SF are described in chapter 3.

Mood Scale

The Mood Scale is a global self-rating assessment of mood (Sperry, 2010). The client is asked to rate his or her mood during the last week on a scale from 0–10, where 0 is the worst mood possible and 10 is the best possible. The mood scale rating is elicited early in each session.

Outcome Rating Scale (ORS)

The Outcome Rating Scale (ORS) (Miller & Duncan, 2000) is a four-item questionnaire used to assess treatment outcomes. The client is asked to make a hatch mark on a 10-centimetier line, indicating how things went in the previous week. The four areas include how the client felt during the past week, the quality of the client's relationships, the client's social and work life, and the client's overall well-being. The ORS is administered before the beginning of each session.

Session Rating Scale (SRS)

The Session Rating Scale (SRS) (Duncan et al., 2003) is a four-item questionnaire used to measure the strength of the therapeutic alliance. Clients are asked how well understood and respected they felt during the session, how satisfied they are with the content of the session, how good a "fit" the therapy approach was, and how satisfied they felt with the session overall. The client is asked to make a hatch mark on a 10-centimeter line, indicating his or her level of agreement with each statement. The SRS is administered near the end of each session and discussed before completing the client leaves. Any score lower than 38 on the SRS is cause for greater attention.

TABLE 5.1 Session 2 Assessment Scores

Patient Health Questionnaire-9 (PHQ-9)	12 (moderate depression)
Outcome Rating Scale (ORS)	20 total: 4 individually, 5 interpersonally, 5 socially, 6 overall
Session Rating Scale (SRS)	38
Mood Scale	4
Therapy outcomes (expected)	Decrease depression (first order goal)
	Shift maladaptive to a more adaptive pattern (second order goal)
	Increased social interest
	Increased motivation and social involvement
MI scores	Importance: 7
	Confidence: 5

Transcription of Session 2

Jennifer completed the PHQ-9 and Outcome Rating Scale (ORS) immediately prior to this session. This session introduces the APFT query sequence to analyze a problematic situation as it relates to Jennifer's maladaptive pattern. Table 5.1 outlines Jennifer's assessment scores and key therapeutic outcomes from the following session.

THERAPIST: Hi Jennifer. It is nice to see you again.

JENNIFER: Thanks. Nice to see you, too.

THERAPIST: Let's start by looking at your mood rating chart from the past week.

JENNIFER: All right. I was able to fill it in each day. There were a couple of hours where I forgot, but I was able to go back and fill it in. For the most part, I was able to keep track.

THERAPIST: Looking it over, I see you wrote "annoyed" and "tired" a lot. Can you tell me more about that?

JENNIFER: Yes, that's been my main reason for coming here in the first place. Feeling tired and lacking motivation a lot. I was surprised that I wrote "annoyed" so much, though. That's something I didn't realize I felt so often.

THERAPIST: What kinds of situations do you find yourself being annoyed in?

JENNIFER: Um, usually when there's a lot of pressure on me to do things. If I have assignments due and people keep texting me about stuff that isn't important. Things like that.

THERAPIST: So, usually when you feel stressed or overwhelmed, or other people are making demands of you?

JENNIFER: Yes, that's right.

THERAPIST: For this next week, I would like you to add another component to your mood chart and write in what the situation is before you make a note of your mood.

JENNIFER: Okay, I can do that.

Commentary

The mood notations on Jennifer's homework chart match her perfectionistic pattern. Jennifer completed her homework this week but admitted there were some days she forgot to fill in her mood chart so she returned to it to attempt to fill in the blanks. This pleasing behavior is congruent with her maladaptive pattern. For this reason, the therapist praised Jennifer's efforts and highlighted how the pattern emerges when Jennifer feels demands are being made of her, as they were in the homework assignment. It is possible that Jennifer's lack of motivation was triggered by the therapist's demands through the homework assignment.

THERAPIST: How would you rate yourself today on the mood scale from 1–10? **(Mood Scale)**

JENNIFER: I would rate myself a 4.

THERAPIST: Alright, a four. Looking over the ORS you just filled out, I see the areas needing the most improvement are individually and socially. Can you tell me more about that? **(ORS review)**

JENNIFER: Yes, individually, I'm still feeling low and sad. (pause) I feel very tired.

THERAPIST: I am sorry to hear that. What about socially?

JENNIFER: I've been having a hard time with school stuff and with seeing other people. That was still my highest score because overall things weren't so good.

THERAPIST: I see you marked socially as the highest but overall it is still pretty low. Can you tell me more about that?

JENNIFER: Sure. I just felt tired all week. I kept feeling guilty because I have so much to do but I felt like I was dragging all week. I barely got enough work done. On Tuesdays, I usually go to a study group. It's very helpful and I like the people there; some of us have hung out outside of the study time. But I was feeling so blah on Tuesday, I didn't even go.

THERAPIST: I understand. I'm sorry to hear you didn't feel up to going, even though you usually enjoy the group. The symptoms you described also match your PHQ-9 score of 12 today. Can you describe a recent situation that was troubling?

Commentary

Because of Jennifer's low ORS scores and her PHQ-9 score indicating moderate depression, this session's query sequence focuses on all three ORS areas—individually, interpersonally, and socially. The situation that Jennifer will describe involves her lack of motivation, self-criticism, and decreased social interest. The query sequence is tailored to these symptoms. The steps of the sequence are indicated in parentheses.

JENNIFER: Yeah. One of my friends from the study group texted me and asked if I was okay. That was nice, but I also felt embarrassed that I was so unproductive.

THERAPIST: So, you felt embarrassed that you didn't go?

JENNIFER: Yes, I could really have used the help studying this week. We are covering some material that is really challenging. I should have gone. But I just could not bring myself to get up and go. I didn't want to get ready and all that. I just stayed home and watched TV.

THERAPIST: Okay, I understand. You usually enjoy and benefit from this study group, but this week you were feeling too tired and unmotivated to go. You stayed home and watched TV instead, but then you felt guilty for not being as productive as you had hoped. Did I get that right?

JENNIFER: Yes, that's right.

THERAPIST: Is that all of what happened? **(1)**

JENNIFER: Yes, that's pretty much it.

THERAPIST: Do you think this might be related to that pattern we discussed of you being perfectionistic and overly conscientious, even when it gets in the way of you being effective with the tasks you set out to do?

JENNIFER: I think it might be. I had a lot of worries about not being able to do the work or participate to the level I would like. So, I figured, what's the point anyway? You know?

THERAPIST: Okay. So, one of your thoughts during this situation was, "What's the point anyway?" **(2)**

JENNIFER: Yes.

THERAPIST: I understand. What else might you have been thinking?

JENNIFER: Um, I thought the people at the study group are going to realize I'm not prepared. They know that I usually do really well, so I didn't want them to look at me like, "What is wrong with her?"

THERAPIST: You worried they would judge you?

JENNIFER: Yes.

THERAPIST: Okay, so your second thought was something like, "They're going to realize I'm not prepared and judge me."

JENNIFER: Yes, that's right. I hate not being prepared.

THERAPIST: Okay, was there another thought?

JENNIFER: I just thought I really messed this up. I was mad at myself.

THERAPIST: So, your thoughts were "What's the point anyway," "They're going to see I'm unprepared and judge me," and "I really messed this up."

JENNIFER: Yes, that's pretty much it.

THERAPIST: Okay. Now that we have identified some of your thoughts during the situation, can we identify some of your behaviors? What did you do during this situation when you were deciding whether to go to the group? **(3)**

JENNIFER: Um, it's more of what I didn't do. I didn't get my work ready.

THERAPIST: You didn't get your work ready.

JENNIFER: Yeah. I also didn't bother showering and getting dressed.

THERAPIST: Okay, so you also did not get yourself ready. Was there anything else?

JENNIFER: Yes, I just watched TV in my sweatpants instead.

THERAPIST: Okay, so I hear you saying you were very tired, so you did not prepare you work or get yourself ready to go. So, you stayed home and watched TV.

JENNIFER: Yes, that's right.

THERAPIST: Ok. Can you tell me what you would have liked to get from this situation? **(4)**

JENNIFER: Yes. I should have gone. That would have been the best thing. It probably would have made me feel better.

THERAPIST: So, what you would have liked was to go to and participate in the study group?

JENNIFER: Yes.

THERAPIST: I think that is a reasonable desired outcome and I agree it may have helped you feel better.

JENNIFER: Yes, probably. It would have helped to at least do something. I wish I felt more motivated.

THERAPIST: Okay, and what was it that actually happened? **(5)**

JENNIFER: Like I said, I didn't go. I just sat around watching TV and I ended up feeling guilty about it. I never even got dressed that day.

THERAPIST: Okay, so you would have liked to go to the study group but what actually happened was that you did not get ready and instead of going you watched TV at home, which made you feel guilty.

JENNIFER: Yes, that's right.

THERAPIST: Would you say you got what you wanted then? **(6)**

JENNIFER: No, of course not.

THERAPIST: Okay, I can see how what happened is related to that pattern where you want to do something well and it gets in the way of you completing the task. Would you agree with that?

JENNIFER: Yes, that's a really good way to put it. That is exactly what happens. And it seems to happen a lot. I will put so much pressure on myself to make something turn out the right way, to do it without any mistakes, and then it's too much pressure and I start thinking what I want is not possible.

THERAPIST: So, that desire to get everything right and make no mistakes becomes too overwhelming and actually interferes with you doing what you want?

JENNIFER: Yes, that's what happens.

THERAPIST: Okay, I understand that. So, would you like to go over this situation, and see how it may have turned out differently for you. How does that sound? **(7)**

JENNIFER: That sounds good. I really don't like how it did turn out.

THERAPIST: Okay. Well, you said your initial thought was, "What's the point anyway." Did thinking that help you or hurt you in getting what you wanted, which was to go to the study group? **(8)**

JENNIFER: I think it hurt me.

THERAPIST: It hurt you. How so?

JENNIFER: Well, after that I felt discouraged. I could only focus on what I was doing wrong.

THERAPIST: Okay, so it made you focus on what you were doing wrong and discouraged you?

JENNIFER: Yes.

THERAPIST: What do you think would have been a more helpful thought in that instance?

JENNIFER: Umm. I could have thought I might not be where I want with my work, but I can still get a lot out of the group.

THERAPIST: Okay, so you could still get some benefit from the study group?

JENNIFER: Yes. I mean that's the point of the study group. It's to help you get prepared.

THERAPIST: So, in reality you don't have to come to the group as prepared as you would have wanted?

JENNIFER: No, not really.

THERAPIST: Then how would that thought have been more helpful to you?

JENNIFER: Um. I think it would have improved my motivation and helped me see the good part of going to the study group.

THERAPIST: Okay, then you would have focused on how the study group would be helpful for you?

JENNIFER: Yes, I think so.

THERAPIST: Good. Now, your second thought was that the people in the group would realize you were not prepared and judge you. Do you think that thought helped you or hurt you in getting to the study group?

JENNIFER: I think that thought hurt me.

THERAPIST: Okay, it hurt you. How so?

JENNIFER: It made me focus on all the stuff I thought I did wrong instead of the things I did right.

THERAPIST: Sort of like the first thought?

JENNIFER: Yes.

THERAPIST: What do you think would have been a more helpful thought?

JENNIFER: I think if I thought they're probably not that prepared either. I'm usually very prepared so I would probably be more prepared than they are anyway.

THERAPIST: It sounds like you weren't giving yourself enough credit.

JENNIFER: Yeah, if I gave myself more credit that would help. I probably wouldn't need to compare myself to them either.

THERAPIST: Not comparing yourself to them. Realizing that you are typically prepared. How would that thought have helped you get to the study group?

JENNIFER: It would have made me feel less overwhelmed. And probably be more reassuring that I can do it and I'm doing well.

THERAPIST: That makes sense. It would have been more reassuring. And probably more accurate.

JENNIFER: Yes, probably more accurate. I often don't give myself enough credit.

THERAPIST: Now, your third thought was, "I really messed this up." Did that thought help you or hurt you get to the study group?

JENNIFER: It didn't help.

THERAPIST: It didn't help. How so?

JENNIFER: I started beating myself up. It's hard to get motivated and focus when I do that.

THERAPIST: Okay, so it's hard to get motivated and focus when you are beating yourself up for not doing things up to your standards?

JENNIFER: Yes, definitely. That's a good way to put it. I don't often realize that is what is happening.

THERAPIST: Right, that makes sense. That is why going through the situation like this can be so helpful because we don't always realize these things when we form a pattern and get used to doing things the same way.

JENNIFER: That makes sense.

THERAPIST: So, what do you think would have been a more helpful thought?

JENNIFER: Well, again, if I didn't focus on the things I thought I did wrong. Maybe if I thought, "I'm doing reasonably well and going to the study group will help me feel even more prepared."

THERAPIST: Focusing on what you're doing well and that the group will help you be better?

JENNIFER: Yes.

THERAPIST: How would that thought have been more helpful?

JENNIFER: It could have helped me get out of my head and focus on what I wanted.

THERAPIST: I agree with that. So, let's move on to your behaviors. Your first behavior was that you didn't prepare your work. Did that behavior help you or hurt you in getting what you wanted, which was to go to the study group? **(9)**

JENNIFER: It hurt me.

THERAPIST: How so?

JENNIFER: Well, then I started falling behind and felt even more sluggish.

THERAPIST: So, it made you feel more sluggish?

JENNIFER: Yes.

THERAPIST: What do you think would have been a more helpful behavior?

JENNIFER: I could have just grabbed my work. Or even gotten it together in advance.

THERAPIST: Getting your work together anyway?

JENNIFER: Yeah.

THERAPIST: How would that have been more helpful?

JENNIFER: It would have probably helped me feel more prepared. Instead of doing the all-or-nothing thing.

THERAPIST: Feeling more prepared would have helped you go?

JENNIFER: Yes, I would have felt readier to go.

THERAPIST: Yes, it sounds like that pattern again.

JENNIFER: Yes, if it's not the way I want it to be, sometimes I won't do it at all. I think just doing my best anyway would have been better.

THERAPIST: It sounds like you're seeing that sometimes your desire to do something up to your high standards puts so much pressure on you that it interferes with you doing the task at all?

JENNIFER: Yes, that happens. I see that more now.

THERAPIST: That's good. And your second behavior was that you did not get dressed and ready to go. Did that help you or hurt you in going to the study group?

JENNIFER: It hurt me. I just felt more tired.

THERAPIST: It made you feel more tired. So maybe this pattern is also contributing to your mood and some of your lack of motivation?

JENNIFER: (Pause) Probably. That really makes sense that what I'm doing contributes to me feeling tired. Or even defeated.

THERAPIST: Yes, I would agree. What do you think would have been more helpful to you in that situation?

JENNIFER: Just getting ready. Maybe choosing a nice outfit.

THERAPIST: Okay, that sounds good. So how would getting ready and choosing a nice outfit have helped you go to the study group?

JENNIFER: I think it would have helped me feel readier and look forward to going out.

THERAPIST: Okay, it would have helped you look forward to it.

JENNIFER: Yes.

THERAPIST: Now, your third behavior was that you stayed home and watched TV. Was that behavior helpful or hurtful?

JENNIFER: That was hurtful also.

THERAPIST: How was it hurtful?

JENNIFER: Well, even though I wasn't going to the group at that point, I thought I would rest up by watching TV, but I really felt more tired afterwards.

THERAPIST: So, you feel more tired?

JENNIFER: Yes.

THERAPIST: What do you think would be a more helpful behavior?

JENNIFER: I think just doing something. Maybe going for a walk or something.

THERAPIST: Okay, so staying active instead?

JENNIFER: Yes.

THERAPIST: I agree. These are very good alternatives. Do you see these as realistic alternatives that you can implement?

JENNIFER: Yes, I think so. (pause) I can see now that those would have helped.

THERAPIST: Good. And it seems you are noticing how doing small things can have a positive effect, rather than the all-or-nothing behavior, as you described?

JENNIFER: Yes, I mean if I got a little active. It doesn't have to be perfect. If I did some of those things, I think it would be more helpful.

THERAPIST: Well, I am glad we were able to process this situation and come up with some good alternatives.

JENNIFER: Me too.

Commentary

Jennifer was very responsive to the query sequence. Her agreeableness and following along is congruent with her conscientious and pleasing pattern. She was able to gain insight into how her perfectionistic pattern affects not only her behaviors, but also her mood. Jennifer begins to understand that when she engages in negative self-talk in relation to her perfectionistic standards, she decreases her own motivation and ability to focus. The therapist reinforces how the query sequence can help Jennifer become more aware and in control of her pattern. This is important because it not only builds credibility in the intervention but gives Jennifer the sense of control she craves and teaches her she can exercise this control in a manner that is more productive and adaptive.

The behaviors Jennifer reported during the query sequence were all passive and involved her withdrawing from the situation. These are consistent with a moderate level of depression, particularly her symptoms of lack of motivation and social isolation. Jennifer's behaviors are also reflective of her lack of a sense of belonging as well as low level of social interest. It is expected that if she can use the replacement behaviors that she generated, her future ORS scores and

SII-SF scores will reflect this change. Jennifer also gained insight into how her self-imposed pressure affects her and reflects her obsessive-compulsive pattern as she not only moves against but moves against herself. Toward the end of step 9, Jennifer begins to make a case for why she should become more active as well as why she does not need to strive for perfection. Her response indicates a decrease in symptoms across the duration of the session, indicated by increased motivation and the beginning of a shift toward a more adaptive pattern.

THERAPIST: Now, since we have been talking about this pattern of keeping yourself from effectively completing your tasks because you are focused on not making mistakes, on a scale from 0 to 10, where 0 is not at all and 10 is the most, how important is it for you to change this pattern? **(10)**

JENNIFER: I would say a 7.

THERAPIST: Okay, so it's quite important?

JENNIFER: Yes, especially now that I see how it holds me back from doing what I want.

THERAPIST: Good. Now on the same 0–10 scale, how confident would you say you are that you can change this pattern?

JENNIFER: Um, maybe 5. It can be very hard and I'm not very confident in making change.

THERAPIST: That is understandable. It can be difficult to change after doing something for a while. But it is very possible. A five is halfway there and that's good. What do you think it would take to move that to a 6 or a 7?

JENNIFER: I think if I'm able to reassure myself that I'm doing well. Focus on the positive stuff like we talked about when that comes up again.

THERAPIST: Okay, so practicing some of the thoughts and behaviors we went over in the session today?

JENNIFER: Yes, I think that will be helpful.

Commentary

Jennifer states she is motivated but hesitant to change her pattern. She reports, however, that she is not very confident she can do it. The therapist is nonjudgmental and helps Jennifer figure out strategies that can improve her confidence. Had the therapist taken a more forceful approach here, it may have triggered Jennifer's maladaptive pattern. Jennifer's importance rating was 10 in the first session, compared to 7 in session two. This probably reflects Jennifer's people-pleasing pattern. Her ability to report the lower score in this session indicates the increasing therapeutic alliance; that is, she feels sufficiently accepted that she can risk not pleasing her therapist by giving an overly high rating.

THERAPIST: I am glad to hear that. So, before we end for today let's spend a few minutes on how you can get the energy and motivation to put these alternatives into practice.

JENNIFER: Okay, that sounds good. I would like to have more energy.

THERAPIST: Good. Sometimes when people have some of the symptoms you described—low mood, loss of pleasure in activities—they stop doing things they once enjoyed. That can lead to a cycle of inactivity, where the less someone does, the less energy and motivation they can muster to do things.

JENNIFER: Yes, that makes sense. I can see that.

THERAPIST: Right, like what you just mentioned about getting active. So, the technique I would like for you to try is called behavioral activation, or acting "as if." What that means is by intentionally becoming more active or activated, you'll start to feel more energy and less depressed. Becoming activated with positive behaviors activates your physiology and you'll start being better. Another way of saying that is that by acting "as if," you are energetic and start moving, and you will become more energetic and feel better. Does that make sense?

JENNIFER Yeah. It does. But is it really that simple?

THERAPIST: Surprisingly, it is. If it's done right. (Pause) I'm going to help you schedule some activities to start. At first, you don't want to take on anything too intense. For example, it is much better to walk just around the block than to plan to run three miles and not do it. Even a small activity can have a big effect.

JENNIFER: Yeah, I've heard about stuff like that when it comes to exercising. You shouldn't take on too much at once.

THERAPIST: Right. So, I'd like to start by scheduling two activities that you can complete this week. Aim for something you can do in about 15 to 20 minutes. What are some things you usually enjoy doing?

JENNIFER: Well, I like to do yoga. And I play the flute. That's something that usually makes me feel good, but I have been totally neglecting it. I also like to go swimming. And have these monthly dinners with a group of friends.

THERAPIST: That sounds good. Playing the flute sounds like it is soothing.

JENNIFER: It is.

THERAPIST: I am glad to hear there are enjoyable activities in your life. You can also look at this list of activities people commonly enjoy. That helps give people more ideas. What stands out to you from that list?

JENNIFER: This list does give me some ideas. I like the idea of taking a bath, going to the park, and working on a collection. I have a collection of gems and minerals I got from different places. I have bunch that I wanted to label and organize.

THERAPIST: Oh wow, that sounds interesting. Have you gone to those gem and mineral shows?

JENNIFER: Yes, I went to one last year. I have these new ones from that. I've been putting it off for a year. I don't know why, because I like doing it.

THERAPIST: Good! Do you think that is something you would like to start with?

JENNIFER: Yes, I could do that for 20 minutes this week.

THERAPIST: Which day of the week will you be doing that?

JENNIFER: Probably Thursday. I have some time off.

THERAPIST: Okay, good. What about a backup if for some reason you cannot complete that activity?

JENNIFER: Um, there is a book I wanted to read for pleasure. I can read that for 15 or 20 minutes.

THERAPIST: That's great. Now what about a second activity?

JENNIFER: Um, maybe taking a bath. Someone got me some fancy bath stuff for my birthday a month ago, but I haven't used it yet.

THERAPIST: Okay, that's good. And that should take you about 15 to 20 minutes

JENNIFER: Yes.

THERAPIST: And what day do you think you will do that?

JENNIFER: I think Friday is good.

THERAPIST: Great. Do you have a backup for that activity?

JENNIFER: I think reading the book is a good backup for this one, too.

THERAPIST: Good. So, you are going to sort your gem and mineral collection for about 20 minutes on Thursday and take a bath with your new products on Friday. That sounds like a good start. You may keep the list of pleasant activities, so you can reference it as needed.

JENNIFER: Okay.

THERAPIST: I am also going to give you this log, so you can track your progress. I want you to write the date and the scheduled activity. Then I want you to give each activity two ratings, on a scale from 0 to 10. The first is how much you completed the activity, whether not at all, somewhat, or completely. You can rate that from 0 to 10. Then, I would like you to rate how much pleasure you got from the activity from 0 to 10, with 0 being none and 10 being the most possible. How does that sound?

JENNIFER: That sounds good. It seems simple enough.

THERAPIST: Okay, I'm glad to hear that. I anticipate you should find some relief with this.

JENNIFER: I hope so.

THERAPIST: Okay, now if you can just fill out the SRS form so we can see if you have been getting what you want out of our meetings. **(SRS review)**

JENNIFER: Okay.

THERAPIST: Okay, I see you were satisfied with our session today and we covered what you wanted to talk about.

JENNIFER: Yes, I think it's going well. I feel a bit better now than when I came in today.

THERAPIST: I am glad to hear that. I look forward to hearing about your progress next time we meet.

Commentary

Jennifer was very agreeable to using the behavioral activation intervention. Her active role in understanding the intervention and planning activities reflects the symptom improvement that occurred during this session. It is also consistent with her need to please authority figures. Jennifer's SRS score both reflects her pattern and confirms her improvement over the session, as she indicates she feels better than when the session began.

Concluding Note

The query sequence is introduced in this session with the goal of using replacement to shift the client from a maladaptive pattern to a more adaptive one. Behavioral activation, a variant of the acting "as if" techniques is also introduced. Starting in this and in subsequent sessions it becomes a key intervention for addressing Jennifer's presenting problem of low mood and loss of interest and pleasure. The therapist continues to assess the client using the Mood Scale and Outcomes Rating Scale. The Session Rating Scale is used to monitor the quality of the therapeutic relationship.

References

Carich, M. (1997). Variations of the "as if" technique. In J. Carlson. & S. Slavik, (Eds.), *Techniques in Adlerian psychology* (pp. 153–160). Washington DC: Accelerated Development.

Carlson, J., Watts, R. E., & Maniacci, M. (2006). *Adlerian therapy: Theory and process.* Washington DC: American Psychological Association.

Duncan, B., Miller, S., Parks, L., Claud, D., Reynolds, L., Brown, J., & Johnson, L. (2003). The Session Rating Scale. Preliminary properties of a "working" alliance measure. *Journal of Affective Disorders, 49*, 59–72.

Hatfield, D. R., McCullough, L., Frantz, S. H., & Krieger, K. (2010). Do we know when our clients get worse? An investigation of therapists' ability to detect negative client change. *Clinical Psychology & Psychotherapy*, 17(1), 25–32.

McCullough, J. (2000). *Treatment for chronic depression: Cognitive behavioral analysis system of psychotherapy.* New York, NY: Guilford.

McCullough, J., Schramm, E., & Penberthy, K. (2014). *CBASP as a distinctive treatment for persistent depressive disorder: Distinctive features.* New York, NY: Routledge.

Meier, S. T. (2015). *Incorporating progress monitoring and outcome assessment into counseling and psychotherapy—A primer.* New York, NY: Oxford University Press.

Miller, S., & Duncan, B. (2002). *The Outcome Rating Scale.* Chicago, IL: Author.

Persons, J. B., & Mikami, A. Y. (2002). Strategies for handling treatment failure successfully. *Psychotherapy: Theory/Research/Practice/Training, 39*(2), 139–151.

Sperry, L. (2005). A therapeutic interviewing strategy for effective counseling practice: Applications to health issues in individual and couples therapy. *The Family Journal: Counseling and Therapy for Couples and Families*, 13 (4), 477–481.

Sperry, L. (2010). *Highly effective therapy: Developing essential clinical competencies in counseling and psychotherapy.* New York, NY: Routledge.

Sperry, L. (2018). Achieving evidence-based status for Adlerian therapy: Why it is needed and how to accomplish it. *Journal of Individual Psychology, 74*(3), 247–264.

6

Session Three

Learning Objectives

In this chapter, you will learn the following:

1. How to incorporate the Adlerian ABC model into the therapeutic process
2. How to continue focusing sessions to facilitate pattern replacement
3. How to continue monitoring client change and homework completion
4. Continuing case of how Adlerian pattern-focused therapy is practiced

The third session of Adlerian pattern-focused therapy continues to stress symptom reduction, enhancement of the therapeutic alliance, and pattern replacement. After reviewing assessment instrument scores and homework assignments with the client, the therapist employs the core therapeutic query sequence with a focus on the client's maladaptive pattern. In the illustrative case, Jennifer is introduced to the Adlerian ABC model to further her understanding of how her thoughts are related to her moods. Finally, the therapist and client agree to continue the acting "as if" variant of behavioral activation, as well as the mood log homework assignment. The chapter begins with a description of the ABC model and then is illustrated in the session transcription that follows.

Adlerian ABC Model

The ABC model is a model for teaching individuals to analyze their behaviors in ABC terms, in which (A) is the antecedent or activating event; (B) is the resulting belief about the activating event; and (C) are the consequences to the behavior or the emotional consequences to the belief. Initially proposed by Albert Ellis (Ellis & Harper, 1975), Ellis formally gave Alfred Adler credit for the ideas behind the model.

> Rational emotive psychology holds to an A-B-C theory of personality.... Adler (1931) put the A-B-C or S-O-R theory of human disturbance very neatly: 'No experience is a cause of success or failure.... We are self-determined by the meaning we give to our experiences; and there is probably something of a mistake always involved when we take particular experiences as the basis of our future life. Meanings are not determined by situations, but we determine ourselves by the meanings we give to situations.' In his book on Individual Psychology, Adler's motto was *omni ex opionione suspense sunt* (everything depends on opinion). I would be hard put to state the essential tenets of RET [now REBT] more succinctly and accurately. (Ellis, 1973, pp. 167–168)

Many Adlerian therapists find that the model "blends well with Adlerian concepts" (McKay & Christianson, 1997, p. 414) and find it useful in their work. In this book, we refer to it as the Adlerian ABC model wherein "B" refers to both belief and behavior.

TABLE 6.1 Session 3 Assessment Scores

Patient Health Questionnaire-9 (PHQ-9)	10 (mild depression)
Outcome Rating Scale (ORS)	22 total: 5 individually, 6 interpersonally, 5 socially, and 5 overall
Session Rating Scale (SRS)	38
Mood Scale	6
Therapy outcomes (expected)	Decrease depression (first order goal)
	Shift maladaptive pattern to an adaptive one (second order goal)
	Increased social interest
	Increased motivation and social involvement
MI scores	Importance: 8
	Confidence: 6

Transcription of Session 3

Jennifer completed the PHQ-9 and Outcome Rating Scale (ORS) immediately prior to this session. In this session, homework is reviewed, and the query sequence is used to move Jennifer toward a more adaptive pattern. Further homework is then assigned. Table 6.1 outlines Jennifer's assessment scores and key therapeutic outcomes from the following session.

THERAPIST: Hi, Jennifer. It's nice to see you again.

JENNIFER: Thank you. Nice to see you, too.

THERAPIST: Why don't we start with a review of your mood rating chart? **(mood chart review)**

JENNIFER: It was pretty similar to last week's, but this week I did write in what the situation was at different times of the day, like you told me to. I still felt irritable, annoyed, and tired a lot. It usually happened when I was thinking about an assignment or someone was bothering me or stressing me out.

THERAPIST: The mood chart is helping you see what triggers some of your emotions, and it's often pressure from school or other people that triggers these negative feelings. Is that right?

JENNIFER: Yes, that seems like that's what it is.

THERAPIST: Can you give me an example of one of the times you felt irritated or annoyed this last week?

JENNIFER: Sure. On Monday, I woke up and felt okay. But then I checked my phone and e-mail and I got a bunch of texts and e-mails from classmates all asking each other about an assignment. I couldn't keep up with them all. It was driving me crazy. I wasn't ready to tackle that assignment yet because I had something else to finish and I didn't want to be bombarded with all these questions and information at once. That's when I wrote "irritated!" with an exclamation point on my mood chart.

THERAPIST: You felt overwhelmed by all the texts and e-mails about this assignment and that led to you feeling irritated.

JENNIFER: Yes.

THERAPIST: I want to tell you about something we call the ABC model. In this model, the A stands for activating event. Those are the things that happen to and around us. The B stands for our beliefs or thoughts about the event. And the C stands for consequences, the emotional and behavioral consequences that result. The model is useful in helping us understand how our emotions are caused by the middle part, the beliefs we have about events, rather than the events themselves. Does that make sense? **(ABC model)**

JENNIFER: Yes (pause). It's like shorthand for understanding where my feelings come from.

THERAPIST: Many find it helpful, and hopefully you will, too. (I hope so, too). What were some of your thoughts when you were receiving all those texts and e-mails from your classmates?

JENNIFER: I thought, "Why are they bothering me?" and "This is not what I need right now."

THERAPIST: Then, in this situation, the A, or activating event, would be the texts and e-mails about the assignment. The B, or beliefs and thoughts, would be "Why are they bothering me?" and "This is not what I need right now." And the C, or emotional consequence, would be your feeling irritated.

JENNIFER: I see. That makes sense. If I'm telling myself they're bothering me and I don't need this right now, then it's like I'm throwing fuel on the fire. I'm letting it irritate me.

THERAPIST: Right. What do you think would have been a more helpful alternative thought?

JENNIFER: Maybe if I thought the information I receive will end up being useful when I actually look at the assignment. When I'm ready to do it.

THERAPIST: Good. Now that you have learned more about how your thoughts are connected to your moods, you can get a better understanding of the alternatives we generate when we review situations.

JENNIFER: That's true. I didn't think about that last time.

Commentary

It was helpful to introduce the ABC model after reviewing Jennifer's mood chart from the last week. Jennifer revealed several thoughts and feelings that are reflective of her maladaptive pattern, and through the ABC model, she was able to gain some insight into how her thoughts and moods are related. While this interaction involved some analysis of the thoughts and their validity, the core replacement strategy was still utilized. This technique also gave Jennifer the tools to implement alternative thoughts on her own.

THERAPIST: I see from your ORS today that there has been some improvement for you personally but you still aren't where you would like to be socially. **(ORS review)**

JENNIFER: Yes, I have been feeling a little better, but I'm still struggling with doing my work and participating in everything I need to be doing.

THERAPIST: I understand that. We will continue to address that in our session today. How have you been feeling on the mood scale. **(Mood Scale)**

JENNIFER: I would say 6 for the last week.

THERAPIST: Alright. Let's look at your activity log from the last week.

JENNIFER: Okay, that sounds fine.

THERAPIST: Okay, so your scheduled activities were taking a bath and sorting your gem and mineral collection. Let's start with the first activity. I see you rated completing that one as a 10. That is great!

JENNIFER: Yes, I completed that.

THERAPIST: And what was your rating for how pleasurable the activity was?

JENNIFER: It was 7. It was good, very relaxing.

THERAPIST: Seven is very good. Can you tell me what you found good about this activity?

JENNIFER: Well, I really like the new cosmetics my friend got me. She is really into beauty products and so she knows what to pick out. The fragrance was very nice. And the hot water loosened my muscles. My back was feeling sore.

THERAPIST: That all does sound very good. Can you tell me what was not so good about the activity?

JENNIFER: Um. Probably when I was in the tub, I could see all the spots in the bathroom that need to be cleaned. That stressed me out.

THERAPIST: You mean you had a different angle from the tub?

JENNIFER: Yeah. And I could see all the spots I never cleaned on the tile.

THERAPIST: Okay, was there anything else?

JENNIFER: Not really.

THERAPIST: Ok, so your second activity, sorting your gems and minerals. How much did you complete that?

JENNIFER: I only completed that about a 6.

THERAPIST: That is still pretty good. How did you enjoy it?

JENNIFER: I rated it a 5. There were things I liked, but it sort of stressed me out.

THERAPIST: Okay, can you tell me what you found good about the activity?

JENNIFER: Yeah. I actually really liked looking at some of the specimens I picked up at the last mineral show. Some of them are so unique. I have a few that are one mineral embedded in another. They are really amazing.

THERAPIST: Wonderful. That sounds very cool. What else was enjoyable about that activity?

JENNIFER: Um. It was very peaceful. It's kind of meditative to sort through and examine that stuff.

THERAPIST: Good. I can see how that would be very relaxing. Now, what was not so good about that activity?

JENNIFER: Well, I was just upset that I didn't finish what I wanted to do. I found one specimen I didn't recognize and I started looking though all these books and online trying to figure it out. It actually took an hour. I'm still not sure about it, but then I spent all that time and I only labeled three pieces.

THERAPIST: Okay, how did you feel about that?

JENNIFER: I felt disappointed because I had started really looking forward to this and when I was done, I still had this big pile left. I barely did any of it, yet I still spent a lot of my time. It was very frustrating.

THERAPIST: Yes, I can hear how frustrating and upsetting it must have been for you.

JENNIFER: Yes, it was upsetting.

THERAPIST: Has this kind of thing happened for you before?

JENNIFER: Oh yes! I mean, it's not always a problem, but sometimes I feel I get carried away trying to fix some small detail that I miss the big picture. Or, that's all I will do. I might actually put off other things because there's something I didn't get right, like on my assignments. Things like that.

THERAPIST: So, sometimes when you have work to do, you find yourself getting so caught up on a minor detail that you are unable to finish the rest of the work?

JENNIFER: Yeah. Or, I will finish the work but then I'll still keep thinking about that one thing I didn't do.

THERAPIST: I understand. In your estimation, what do you think keeps you focused on those details, even when you know it isn't very productive?

JENNIFER: Um, I think just that I want stuff to be done correctly. I don't like to do a sloppy job.

THERAPIST: That is very admirable.

JENNIFER: Thank you.

THERAPIST: Although maybe not so helpful in situations like the one you just described?

JENNIFER: No, not at all.

THERAPIST: Would you say that's related to your pattern of being perfectionistic that interferes with you accomplishing certain tasks?

Commentary

Jennifer was not fully compliant with completing her behavioral activation homework this week since both activities triggered her maladaptive pattern. While she was able to manage it more effectively during the first exercise and did not interrupt her bath to clean the tile, the second activity proved more challenging. In this case, Jennifer's nonadherence to her assignment proved helpful because it allowed for processing of the maladaptive pattern. As Jennifer discussed her homework assignment, she appeared frustrated, an indication of how her pattern triggers her mood. Her maladaptive pattern was likely triggered in this interchange but the therapist was able to effectively address the pattern by being supportive but still illustrate how although the pattern can be helpful in some situations, it is ultimately unhelpful when left unchecked. The following query sequence is tailored to Jennifer's ORS score, Mood Scale score, and reaction to her homework assignments, as it addresses her perfectionistic pattern and the frustration and down mood resulting from it. The steps in the following query sequence are noted in parentheses.

JENNIFER: Oh, yes. I would definitely say that. (Pause) There was something else that happened this last week along the same lines.

THERAPIST: Alright, would you like to tell me about it? **(1)**

JENNIFER: Yes, actually. It was pretty stressful. I had a paper due that I had put off. So, I was doing it a couple of days before it was due. I managed to finish it in time, even though I wasn't sure I would. But then when I was going to turn it in, I was rereading it and I noticed that I wrote the wrong thing in one part. It was for my political science class and I realized I wrote some wrong information in one part.

THERAPIST: And what was that?

JENNIFER: I used a term incorrectly in one spot. There was a different term I was supposed to use.

THERAPIST: Okay.

JENNIFER: Well, then I could not bring myself to hand in the paper, even though this wasn't a really huge error. I actually went back home to change it and I ended up turning in my paper late, which is even worse.

THERAPIST: Okay. So, you had a paper due and you were about to turn it in when you noticed a relatively small mistake, but you were unable to let the mistake go and went home to change it, which resulted in you turning your paper in late. Is that correct?

JENNIFER: Yes, that's right.

THERAPIST: Is that all of what happened?

JENNIFER: Yes. I told my professor what happened. Hopefully it will turn out okay and I won't lose too many points.

THERAPIST: Okay. So, can you tell me what you were thinking during this situation? What were some of the thoughts you had? **(2)**

JENNIFER: Um, I thought, "If I turn it in like this, I'm going to fail."

THERAPIST: Okay, so you thought, "I'm going to fail if I turn it in like this."

JENNIFER: Yes.

THERAPIST: What else?

JENNIFER: I thought, "This paper is a disaster. I need to go change it."

THERAPIST: Okay, so your other two thoughts were, "This paper is a disaster" and "I need to go change it." Was there anything else?

JENNIFER: Not really.

THERAPIST: Alright. I understand how that must have been stressful for you.

JENNIFER: Yes, very much so. It was a mess.

THERAPIST: Then, what were some of your behaviors? What did you do in this situation? **(3)**

JENNIFER: Well, first off, I caught the mistake because I kept rereading my paper.

THERAPIST: Ah, ok. So, you sort of re-read it a few times to keep checking it?

JENNIFER: Yes.

THERAPIST: What else did you do?

JENNIFER: I didn't turn the paper in. I went home to edit it.

THERAPIST: You did not turn it in when it was due, and you went home to edit the paper. Is that right?

JENNIFER: Yes, that's right.

THERAPIST: So, Jennifer, what were you hoping to get out of this situation? What would have been a good outcome for you? **(4)**

JENNIFER: I think if my professor had just let me edit my paper and turn it in late without taking points off.

THERAPIST: That does sound ideal, but is that something you could control?

JENNIFER: No, I can't make him do that.

THERAPIST: I agree. What do you think would have been a good outcome, in your control, that you would have liked, considering the circumstances?

JENNIFER: I think just turning the paper in on time, even with the mistake. That mistake was small when I look back on it. Then I could have been done and not stressed about it anymore.

THERAPIST: Okay, so you would have liked to get it in in time, regardless of the mistake. And then it would be off your mind?

JENNIFER: Yes. That would have been better.

Commentary

Jennifer initially gave a desired outcome that is not within her control. Her response was indicative of the part of her maladaptive pattern that is criticizing and controlling. By being prompted to consider an outcome that is reasonable and does not involve controlling others, she was able to understand how her criticism is not only self-defeating, but unwarranted. She also replaced her unreasonable desired outcome with a more acceptable and realistic one.

THERAPIST: And what actually happened? **(5)**

JENNIFER: I ended up stressing about it and turning it in late.

THERAPIST: Then you would have liked to turn your paper in on time but you ended up going home to change it and turning it in late.

JENNIFER: Yes.

THERAPIST: So, would you say you got what you wanted? **(6)**

JENNIFER: No, not at all. It actually stressed me out more.

THERAPIST: I understand it must have been stressful to then turn the paper in late after all that work.

JENNIFER: Yes, it was. It was a total disappointment.

THERAPIST: So, would you like to go over this situation again and see how it may have turned out differently? **(7)**

JENNIFER: Sure.

THERAPIST: Okay, good. Let's look at your thoughts and behaviors and see if and they reflect your maladaptive pattern about your thoughts. Your first one was, "I'm going to fail if I turn the paper in like this." Was that thought helpful or hurtful in getting what you wanted, which was to turn your paper in on time? **(8)**

JENNIFER: Um, it was hurtful.

THERAPIST: How so?

JENNIFER: It made me feel like I messed up and like there was no way I could turn that in at the time.

THERAPIST: It sounds like you felt less confident about it.

JENNIFER: Yes, exactly.

THERAPIST: Do you think that could be related to your pattern of being overly conscientious?

JENNIFER: Yes, it definitely is. I have a hard time letting things go when I'm not sure about how well they are.

THERAPIST: Right. And often that gets in the way of you being as effective as you would like?

JENNIFER: Yes, that's definitely true. I can see it in this, just like when I was sorting through my collection.

Commentary

With this comment, Jennifer was able to connect her maladaptive pattern or lifestyle strategy and her various life situations, whether it is completing an assignment or engaging in a pleasurable activity.

THERAPIST: It makes sense then that these unhelpful thoughts are related to that pattern. What do you think might have been a more helpful thought in that situation?

JENNIFER: Maybe if I just thought that I did my best and it's not that big a mistake.

THERAPIST: I understand. You did your best and it's not that big of a mistake. That thought reflects what we will call your adaptive or healthy pattern of being "reasonably conscientious while maintaining effectiveness"? Does that make sense to you?

JENNIFER: (Pause) Yes. I can see that.

THERAPIST: And how would that thought and this more adaptive pattern have helped you turn in the paper on time?

JENNIFER: It would have helped me relax and not freak out about it.

THERAPIST: So, it would have helped you not freak out and not catastrophize the situation?

JENNIFER: Yes, that's a good way to put it. I felt like it was a catastrophe at the time, and now I see it didn't have to be.

Commentary

By introducing the adaptive pattern of being reasonably conscientious while maintaining effectiveness and illustrating how the alternative thought is reflective of this, the therapist helped Jennifer see how the adaptive pattern helps her not only be more effective but also improves her mood. Jennifer introduced the word, "catastrophize" here, which is traditionally associated with cognitive distortions. In this instance, the therapist did not have to help her use logic to analyze or dispute her thoughts, but the focus on her pattern and replacement of thoughts helped Jennifer arrive at this insight on her own. She was able to integrate this information in her processing of the second thought as the query sequence continues.

THERAPIST: Your second thought was, "This paper is a disaster." Did that thought help you or hurt you get what you wanted, which was to turn the paper in on time?

JENNIFER: That hurt me also. That was more of the same—just thinking, "I totally messed this up."

THERAPIST: So, it made you start blaming yourself?

JENNIFER: Yes, exactly. That's what happens when I start thinking like that.

THERAPIST: How do you think that affects your mood?

JENNIFER: (Pause) It definitely makes me more depressed. I feel guilty and like a failure.

THERAPIST: You feel guilty and like a failure when you think that way?

JENNIFER: Yes.

THERAPIST: It makes sense that thinking those things about yourself makes you feel depressed. How do you think that might be related to your pattern of being overly conscientious, even when it gets in the way of you getting what you want?

JENNIFER: I can definitely see that I stress myself out when I think that way. I guess it makes sense that when I feel guilty and like a failure when things aren't just right that I get depressed.

THERAPIST: So, you are seeing a connection between your level of conscientiousness and feeling depressed?

JENNIFER: Yeah, well if I'm trying to make something a certain way and I can't, or if I get super focused on some little detail, then I feel bad and I think I'm going to fail. (Pause) That definitely affects my mood and makes me feel like what's the point.

THERAPIST: So, might it also decrease your motivation?

JENNIFER: (Pause) Yeah, I guess it affects me on a lot of levels. My motivation, my mood, and actually doing the work I want to do.

Commentary

Up to now, the focus on Jennifer's maladaptive pattern has primarily focused on her excessive conscientiousness. However, this interaction demonstrated how the self-critical part of her pattern is tied to her depression.

THERAPIST: That makes sense. What do you think would have been a more helpful thought other than "This paper is a disaster?"

JENNIFER: If I thought that it's just one thing I messed up. The rest of the paper was good.

THERAPIST: How would thinking, "The rest of the paper is good" have helped you turn the paper in on time?

JENNIFER: It would have encouraged me to let go of that minor detail.

THERAPIST: Yes, and perhaps see the good in the work you did.

JENNIFER: Yes, I did work hard on it and there were parts I was proud of.

THERAPIST: Is that a thought you can see yourself having?

JENNIFER: Yes, maybe now that we are talking about it. If I can remember when I am feeling upset in a situation like that.

THERAPIST: Good. That leads us to your third thought, "I have to go change the paper." Did that thought help you or hurt you get what you wanted, which was to turn the paper in on time?

JENNIFER: It hurt me.

THERAPIST: How did that thought hurt?

JENNIFER: Well, then I just became focused on changing it instead of seeing the good, like you said.

THERAPIST: Right, you became focused on what you did not like about it.

JENNIFER: Yes.

THERAPIST: Then what do you think would have been a more helpful thought?

JENNIFER: If I thought, "It's too late now, it's not that big a deal. It's better to turn it in on time than to go back just to change one little thing."

THERAPIST: So, it's better to turn it in on time than to go back and change a detail that might not be that important?

JENNIFER: Yeah. I think that would have helped me just turn it in and move on. I have a lot of other work to do.

THERAPIST: And that would have prompted you to turn it in and move on to your other responsibilities?

JENNIFER: Yes.

THERAPIST: That's a good alternative. It sounds like it would save you a lot of stress and maybe not beat yourself up so much.

JENNIFER: Yes, that's true.

THERAPIST: And more of focusing on the big picture, as you mentioned you would like to do?

JENNIFER: Yeah, that's true. It doesn't help to get stuck on the little things.

THERAPIST: Yes, I agree. Let's move on to your behaviors. Your first behavior was that you kept rereading your paper. Did that behavior help you or hurt you in turning the paper in on time? **(9)**

JENNIFER: It hurt me.

THERAPIST: It hurt. How so?

JENNIFER: It made me start analyzing stuff and overthinking things.

THERAPIST: You found you were overthinking?

JENNIFER: Yes.

THERAPIST: If rereading the paper didn't help, what do you think could have been a more helpful behavior in this situation?

JENNIFER: Probably just turning in the paper and not looking at it again.

THERAPIST: Just turning in the paper?

JENNIFER: Yes.

THERAPIST: How would that have been more helpful?

JENNIFER: It wouldn't let me give myself a chance to second guess myself. I would just turn it in and that's it.

THERAPIST: That sounds good. Is that something you can see yourself doing?

JENNIFER: Yes, I think so. I can just remind myself I'm not going to stress about it.

THERAPIST: Good. Now, your second behavior was to not turn in the paper. Did that hurt your or help your getting it in on time?

JENNIFER: Obviously that hurt.

THERAPIST: Then what would have been an alternative behavior that would have helped you? A behavior that would reflect your more adaptive pattern of "reasonably conscientious while maintaining effectiveness"?

JENNIFER: (Pause) Just hand it in and remind myself I did my best.

THERAPIST: Reminding yourself you did your best and just handing in the paper?

JENNIFER: Yes. Maybe if I just turned it in and didn't give myself time to really overthink it or to look through it for mistakes. Like, just saying that it was done and there was no reason to go back to it.

THERAPIST: It sounds like you're saying you could trust yourself more and handing it in wouldn't allow you time to start overanalyzing it?

JENNIFER: Yes, that seems to be when I get in trouble.

THERAPIST: When you start thinking about something too much?

JENNIFER: Yeah.

THERAPIST: What happens when you start thinking too much about something?

JENNIFER: Well, I can get caught up in trying to make something the way I think it should be. And I usually feel bad about myself—that I messed something up.

THERAPIST: So, that leads to you having a low mood?

JENNIFER: (Pause) Yeah, I guess. It's a pretty bad feeling when I feel I messed something up, especially if I worked hard on it.

THERAPIST: I understand how that must be frustrating.

JENNIFER: It is.

THERAPIST: Okay, now moving on to your last behavior of going back to edit your paper. Did that behavior help you or hurt you in this situation?

JENNIFER: It hurt. Obviously, that's the opposite of what I wanted.

THERAPIST: Right, it's not what you said you would have liked to get out of this situation, which was to turn in your paper on time. What do you think would have been a more helpful behavior?

JENNIFER: Just leave it and turn it in.

THERAPIST: Just leave it and turn it in.

JENNIFER: Yes.

THERAPIST: I agree that would have probably been more helpful. So, as we are discussing this pattern of being so conscientious that it interferes with your other tasks, how important is it to you to change this pattern on a scale from 0 to 10, where 0 is not at all and 10 is the highest? **(10)**

JENNIFER: I would say an 8.

THERAPIST: An 8 is very important.

JENNIFER: Yes. I mean I don't see myself as wanting to change it completely because I think it helps me do things right. But I'm starting to see how it gets in the way.

THERAPIST: So, you are saying you would like to harness some of the good qualities from that pattern but use it to your advantage instead of allowing it to get in your way?

JENNIFER: Yes. I want to be able to do my work well. I just don't want to drive myself crazy about it.

THERAPIST: Okay. Now, on that same 0 to 10 scale, how confident are you that you can change this pattern to being more "reasonably conscientious while maintaining effectiveness"?

JENNIFER: (Pause) Um, I think a 6.

THERAPIST: Okay, that's very good. A 6 is more than halfway. What do you think it would take to move that to a 7 or an 8?

JENNIFER: Maybe if I can do it one time. Like, put the paper away or just hand it in.

THERAPIST: Okay, so if you had a little practice?

JENNIFER: Yes, that would help.

THERAPIST: Good. You have come up with some great alternatives analyzing this situation today. What was your take on that?

JENNIFER: It was okay. It was good that it helped me see how I overanalyze things sometimes. I mean, I already know I do that but I never thought about how it gets in the way of things or how it makes me sad or depressed.

THERAPIST: It sounds like you were able to gain a different perspective from this.

JENNIFER: Yeah, just talking about it I started to realize how stressful it is.

Commentary

Jennifer seems to have gained important insights during the query sequence. The therapist helped her understand how her pattern is triggered by certain triggers, which will be useful in creating a future relapse prevention plan. Jennifer also learned how her pattern influences her mood and how thoughts and behaviors that are more reflective of her more adaptive pattern can help her manage her frustration, low mood, and lack of motivation. She appeared to get frustrated toward the end of the query sequence, likely because the self-critical aspect of her pattern was triggered as she processed the unhelpful nature of her behaviors. Her response to the MI questions (step 10) revealed Jennifer's motivation is increasing but her confidence needs improvement. To avoid further triggering Jennifer's pattern, the therapist gently encouraged Jennifer when she revealed some frustration because of overanalyzing situations. Nevertheless, she conceded that the query sequence helped her understand how this behavior affects her mood. This response may be indicative of the people-pleasing aspect of her pattern.

THERAPIST: It does sound stressful. I am glad you were able to see those connections. (Pause). Would you like to move on to scheduling some activities for the upcoming week?

JENNIFER: Sure.

THERAPIST: Good. Did you have any particular activities in mind for this week?

JENNIFER: Um, I'm not sure. I've thought about some things but I really don't know what I want to do.

THERAPIST: Well why don't we start with some of your ideas. What was one idea you had for this week?

JENNIFER: Well, I actually have tickets to a comedy show with some friends. That's more than 15 to 20 minutes so I wasn't sure if that could be one of the activities.

THERAPIST: Yes, that sounds like a great idea. I'm sure it will be a lot of fun. You have been planning on going?

JENNIFER: Yes, we bought the tickets a while ago. I actually forgot about it for a while.

THERAPIST: And what night is that?

JENNIFER: That's on Saturday.

THERAPIST: That sounds good. What is something else you were thinking about doing?

JENNIFER: I was thinking about getting outside since the weather has been getting nice.

THERAPIST: I agree. What are some things you could possibly do outside?

JENNIFER: I guess take a walk.

THERAPIST: Is that something you think you would like?

JENNIFER: Yeah, I used to like taking more walks. I used to walk to the dog park. It's about a five-minute walk from my house and I like seeing the dogs.

THERAPIST: Aw, I'm sure they are cute.

JENNIFER: Yeah. I want to get a dog once I'm out of school.

THERAPIST: It sounds like you can walk to the dog park and that will take you about 15 minutes or so.

JENNIFER: Yes.

THERAPIST: And what day will you schedule that for?

JENNIFER: I think Wednesday is good. Wednesday after class.

THERAPIST: Great. It sounds like fun. How about a backup activity in case the weather prevents you from taking a walk on Wednesday? Is there another way you can fit in some exercise that day?

JENNIFER: Yes, I can walk up and down the stairs in my building. I do that for exercise sometimes.

THERAPIST: That sounds like a good plan. So, Wednesday after class you will take a walk to the dog park, and on Saturday you're going to a comedy show with your friends. I think that sounds like a nice week. I would like you to log these activities and rate them on a scale from 0 to 10 in terms of how much you completed each activity and how much pleasure you derived from each one.

JENNIFER: Okay, I will do that. I was also thinking about trying some other things.

THERAPIST: Great. What have you been thinking about trying?

JENNIFER: Maybe saying something positive to myself. Like, I read an article about a woman who became a self-help writer after she became a widow. She said she starts every day by saying, "Today's going to be a good day!" out loud.

THERAPIST: Okay, so maybe saying something affirming like that out loud each morning?

JENNIFER: Yeah, something like that.

THERAPIST: Starting your day on a positive note might influence how the rest of the day goes.

JENNIFER: Yeah, it could.

THERAPIST: What are some other ideas for things you could do to lift your mood?

JENNIFER: Um, I just had a thought of putting my last economics exam up on my bulletin board because I got 100%.

THERAPIST: Oh, wow, that's very impressive.

JENNIFER: That way I can look at it and maybe feel better.

THERAPIST: Okay, so a way of being reminded of your accomplishments?

JENNIFER: Well, I was very excited when I got my exam back and saw the score because we have been going through some very difficult material and I was nervous about this class because it's a very important prerequisite.

THERAPIST: Putting the test up will allow you to sort of re-experience that good feeling when you look at it?

JENNIFER: Yes. It could.

THERAPIST: Do you have any other ideas that might help?

JENNIFER: Maybe calling some of my friends back home more often. It's really hard to keep in contact because we are all at different schools now and some people are even in different time zones. I do like talking to them, though.

THERAPIST: Connecting with some of your friends from back home might help you feel better.

JENNIFER: It's not stressful. We kind of just laugh about stuff that happened in high school or just be silly.

THERAPIST: That does sound like a fun idea. Of these three ideas, which one do you think might be something you could do that would be helpful in lifting your mood?

JENNIFER: Um, well I have a lot of stuff to do and those other activities we planned, so I don't know when I will have time to call my friends. We play phone-tag a lot so it isn't always easy to get in touch right away.

THERAPIST: So, maybe that is not the best idea right now?

JENNIFER: Probably not.

THERAPIST: What about the other two—saying an affirmation when you wake up or hanging up your test?

JENNIFER: I think probably saying the affirmation is the best because it's easy and I was just thinking if I look at my test too much I might just start thinking about all the stuff I'm not doing, or all the work I have to do and I might end up feeling worse.

THERAPIST: Saying an affirmation will be the most convenient and most likely to work for you right now?

JENNIFER: Yes, I think so.

THERAPIST: I think it's a great idea. It might be more convenient for you to say the same affirmation each morning.

JENNIFER: Okay, I can say it when I get up.

THERAPIST: What would you like the affirmation to be?

JENNIFER: I think if I said, "I'm going to have a good day."

THERAPIST: That's very good. So, when you wake up in the morning, you are going to say, "I'm going to have a good day." There may be times when it feels sort of corny or as though it won't work, but I want you to do it as if it will work.

JENNIFER: Okay, I will try that. It seems easy enough.

Commentary

Indicative of her increasing motivation and on her way to becoming her own therapist (third order change), Jennifer offered some ways in which she could foster change in her life, including affirmations. The therapist supported Jennifer's efforts and encouraged her to choose activities that are likely not to trigger her pattern. Additionally, these social activities are geared toward increasing Jennifer's level of social interest and belonging.

THERAPIST: Good. You accomplished a lot in this session and I look forward to hearing about how everything goes. We will review your progress next time.

JENNIFER: Okay, thank you.

THERAPIST: Okay, so just one thing before we finish. Please fill out this form so we can see if you have been getting what you want out of our session today. **(SRS review)**

JENNIFER: Okay.

THERAPIST: (pause to review and calculate score). Okay, I see you were satisfied with our session today and we covered what you wanted to talk about.

JENNIFER: I really wanted to talk about my school stuff and I think we accomplished that today. I don't feel as guilty about it as I did.

THERAPIST: I am glad to hear that. I look forward to seeing you next time.

Commentary

Although her maladaptive pattern was triggered at several points, Jennifer showed improvement in her mood from the beginning to the end of the session. She reported decreased guilt and her SRS score indicated her satisfaction with the session. While this was a trying session for Jennifer, she felt encouraged and was able to make significant progress, as evidenced by her improved mood and motivation.

Concluding Note

The therapeutic alliance was firmly established by this session, as suggested by a number of indicators. These include the fact that Jennifer returned after the first and second sessions, that she was increasingly engaged in the treatment process during sessions by active involvement and between sessions by doing the mutually agreed-on homework. It also is reflected in her high scores on the Session Rating Scale, which is a formal measure of the therapeutic alliance. These indicators suggest that the therapist was responsive to what Jennifer wanted to discuss and process, that the therapist had an encouraging manner, and that Jennifer believed she was making progress on her goals for therapy.

The therapist continued to employ the query sequence to facilitate pattern change, and ongoing assessment of the therapeutic process continues. The Adlerian ABC model was introduced in the case of Jennifer to help her understand more fully how thoughts and beliefs are connected to behavioral and emotional consequences. Particularly heartening was an early indication of third order change by Jennifer.

References

Ellis, A. (1973). Rational-emotive therapy. In R. J. Corsini (Ed.), *Current psychotherapies* (pp. 167–206). Itasca, IL: F. E. Peacock.

Ellis, A., & Harper, R. (1975). *A new guide to rational living.* North Hollywood, CA: Wilshire.

McKay, G., & Christianson, O. (1997). Helping adults change disjunctive emotional responses to children's misbehavior. In J. Carlson. & S. Slavik, (Eds.), *Techniques in Adlerian psychology* (pp. 413–428). Washington DC: Accelerated Development.

7

Session Four

Learning Objectives

In this chapter, you will learn the following:

1. How to incorporate role playing into Adlerian pattern-focused therapy
2. How to incorporate the reflecting "as if" technique
3. How to continue focusing sessions to increase pattern change
4. How to redirect a client who indicates a desired outcome that is not in his or her control
5. Continuing case of how Adlerian pattern-focused therapy is practiced

Session four marks further change in the therapeutic process. The therapeutic alliance should be well established at this point, with therapists continuing to incorporate Session Rating Scale (SRS) scores into their decision-making process. Session four begins with a review of the client's mood log and behavioral activation assignments, as well as a discussion of Mood Scale and ORS scores. The query sequence is then tailored to problematic concerns identified in the ORS scores, focusing on ameliorating the maladaptive pattern and increasing social interest. Finally, the therapist continues assigning mutually agreed-on homework. In the illustrative case, the therapist helps Jennifer role play a potential scenario, so she can practice her alternative behaviors and increase her confidence in her ability to change her maladaptive pattern. This chapter describes the new therapeutic intervention and presents a full, illustrative case transcription with commentary.

Role Playing

Roleplaying has a long tradition in Adlerian therapy. Based on his experience with various forms of roleplaying, including psychodrama, Raymond Corsini wrote the first book on role playing in individual and group therapy from an Adlerian perspective (Corsini, 1966). As noted in chapter 3, role playing is a variant of the "as if" technique used to help individuals practice new, adaptive behaviors. "The goal of role playing is to generate new behaviors, as the individual enacts an 'as if/what if' problem resolution script" (Carich, 1997, p. 154). Through modeling, practice, and feedback, the therapist helps the client build appropriate social skills. Verbal and nonverbal behaviors are practiced in a role play scenario between the client and therapist. The therapist praises the client's efforts and gives constructive feedback to help improve new skills. In the illustrative case of Jennifer, the therapist employs role play when discussing Jennifer's level of confidence in changing her maladaptive pattern. This gives Jennifer an opportunity to practice her alternative behaviors, and her confidence improves when she sees she is able to respond using her new skills.

Reflecting "As If"

As already noted in chapter 3, the reflecting "as if" technique (Watts, 2003) is another variant of the acting "as if" technique. It is used to help clients reflect on how things would be different if they were already acting in the ways they desired. Like acting "as if", reflecting "as if" involves the replacement strategy. Individuals replace the current way they view themselves and their circumstances with a new way of thinking of themselves and their lives. The therapist guides the client as he or she brainstorms goals for how life could be different and behaviors that could help the client achieve these goals. This intervention has been applied in various contexts including children, team members, and self-injurious clients, (La Guardia, Watts, & Garza, 2013; Watts & Garza, 2008; Watts, & Trusty, 2003).

Transcription of Session 4

This session utilizes APFT to analyze a situation Jennifer recently experienced in terms of her maladaptive pattern. Jennifer completed the PHQ-9 and Outcome Rating Scale (ORS) immediately prior to this session. Role play is used to help Jennifer practice implementing her adaptive pattern and increase her confidence. Reflecting "as if" is used to help Jennifer replace her current thinking about herself with a more adaptive and desirable way of thinking. Table 7.1 outlines Jennifer's assessment scores and key therapeutic outcomes from the following session.

THERAPIST: Hi Jennifer. It is nice to see you again.

JENNIFER: It's nice to see you as well.

THERAPIST: Tell me about your mood chart from this past week. **(mood chart review)**

JENNIFER: I noticed it was a little better overall. One day I wrote "irritated" and "frustrated" nearly the entire day, but the next day was a little better.

THERAPIST: What was going on the day you felt irritated and frustrated?

JENNIFER: I had a lot of homework to do. I was frustrated about a paper I procrastinated on and then I had no idea what I was doing when I started. I was mad that I hadn't started sooner or gone to the library earlier once I realized how much I had to do.

TABLE 7.1 Session 4 Assessment Scores

Patient Health Questionnaire-9 (PHQ-9)	9 (mild depression)
Outcome Rating Scale (ORS)	26 total: 7 individually, 6 interpersonally, 6 socially, 7 overall
Session Rating Scale (SRS)	40
Mood Scale	6
Therapy outcomes (expected)	Decrease depression (first order goal)
	Shift from maladaptive pattern to adaptive one (second order goal)
	Increased social interest
	Increased motivation and social involvement
MI scores	Importance: 9
	Confidence: 7

THERAPIST: All right, you felt frustrated and irritated on a day when you were overwhelmed with work.

JENNIFER: Right, which is what usually happens.

THERAPIST: I understand and remember you mentioning that before. Why don't we review how your activities went last week?

JENNIFER: Okay, my activities were to go to a comedy show and to take a walk. I did both. I have my log right here.

THERAPIST: That's great. Let's start with the first activity, the comedy club. How did you rate that?

JENNIFER: I rated it a 10 for completion and 8 for enjoyment.

THERAPIST: Very good. What was good about this activity?

JENNIFER: It was a lot of fun. The show was really funny, and it put me in a good mood. It was really nice.

THERAPIST: Good. What was not so good about this activity?

JENNIFER: Um, one of my friends was very annoying and she kept commenting about how we should go out after, but I was already tired. And she kept saying, "Oh I never see you anymore." I was offended by that because she doesn't know what's going on and it's none of her business.

THERAPIST: So, she brought up that you haven't been as social lately and that was difficult for you to hear because this has been your own process trying to get out of this rut and other people really don't know or understand what you are going through.

JENNIFER: Yes, that can be really isolating. I finally got out a little and I just didn't want to hear it.

THERAPIST: I understand. And other than that, you enjoyed yourself?

JENNIFER: Yes, I did.

THERAPIST: Your second activity was going for a walk to the park. How was that?

JENNIFER: I rated that a 10 for completion and a 6 for enjoyment.

THERAPIST: Good. What was good about that activity?

JENNIFER: Um, the weather was nice. It was nice to get out for a little bit.

THERAPIST: Then you enjoyed going out and the weather was nice. What was not so good about this activity?

JENNIFER: I don't know. I just didn't feel that great. I still felt depressed. Then I was upset that the walk didn't help. I felt very tired. I had to force myself and I felt like I was really dragging that day.

THERAPIST: Even though you enjoyed parts of this activity, you felt tired and depressed and you were disappointed that the walk didn't help lift your mood as much as you would have liked.

JENNIFER: Yes, that's right. I mean, it was okay. But not that good. I'm glad I did it, but I just felt so tired.

THERAPIST: Let's move on to reviewing your ORS form for today. **(ORS review)**

JENNIFER: Okay, that sounds good.

THERAPIST: Can you tell me more about your rating for how you have been doing individually?

JENNIFER: Sure. That was a little better than last time but still not so great. I feel tired a lot and a lot of things have been getting on my nerves recently.

THERAPIST: I understand, and I hope we can continue to address those concerns. Your rating for interpersonal was quite high. Can you tell me more about that?

JENNIFER: I don't really have a lot of complaints in that area. I guess that's good. That part of my life seems okay right now.

Commentary

Jennifer was able to successfully complete her behavioral activation homework despite several potential obstacles. She rated the first activity an 8 for enjoyment although her friend triggered her pattern, and fully completed the second activity, taking a walk, despite her fatigue. Jennifer's efforts reflected an increased level of motivation. It is increasingly obvious to her that her pattern directly impacts her moods. Additionally, the past week's activities increased Jennifer's social interest and belonging, resulting in decreased mood symptoms, as apparent in her PHQ-9 and ORS scores this week.

THERAPIST: That is good to hear. How would you rate yourself on the mood scale? **(Mood Scale)**

JENNIFER: Overall, I am feeling a little better. About a 6 on the mood scale. The main issue recently has been socially. Just lots of stress with school and my friends.

THERAPIST: I am sorry to hear that. Was there anything pertaining to that that came up recently?

JENNIFER: Yes, I guess so. There was something that made me feel really annoyed and frustrated a couple of days ago.

THERAPIST: I understand. Can you tell me more about what happened? **(1)**

JENNIFER: Sure. My friend won a gift certificate to the movies in a raffle they had at the student center. She could take one person with her and she asked me if I wanted to go. That was nice of her, but she had waited a couple of weeks to ask me and by the time she did, the certificate was valid for only another two weeks. I felt really annoyed that she would drop the ball like that and only give me such a short notice. She knows how busy I am, and I need to plan stuff in advance.

THERAPIST: So, your friend won a gift certificate to the movies and asked you to go but by the time you started making plans there was a short time left to use the certificate and you felt like you were pressed for time. Is that right?

JENNIFER: Yes, that's right. I don't know why she had to neglect it like that.

THERAPIST: Alright, is that all of what happened?

JENNIFER: Yes, that's pretty much it. I didn't agree to go this week, so I guess maybe next week if I can make it.

Commentary

Because Jennifer reported her primary concern on the ORS is social functioning, and her pattern was triggered by one of her friends as she was completing her homework assignment, the query sequence was tailored to these concerns. The situation provided an opportunity to process Jennifer's perfectionistic pattern, including her criticism of others. Analyzing this specific situation is critical at this point as Jennifer has been steadily increasing. If Jennifer is successful in ameliorating her pattern and connecting with others, during the situation presented in the query sequence, her social interest will increase further.

THERAPIST: Can you tell me some of the thoughts you had during this situation? **(2)**

JENNIFER: Yes. I thought she should have asked me when I would be available instead of waiting.

THERAPIST: Now, your thought was she should have asked you?

JENNIFER: Yes.

THERAPIST: What else were you thinking?

JENNIFER: I thought, "Doesn't she realize how busy I am? I have a lot on my plate right now and I can't believe she doesn't realize that I need more notice than that."

THERAPIST: Then your second thought was "Doesn't she realize how busy I am?"

JENNIFER: Yes, I also felt annoyed because she does stuff like this. She doesn't think before she does things.

THERAPIST: So, a third thought was, "She doesn't think before she does things." Is that correct?

JENNIFER: Yes.

THERAPIST: Was there anything else?

JENNIFER: No, I think that was it.

THERAPIST: Okay. Now then, let's move on to your behaviors. What did you do in this situation? **(3)**

JENNIFER: Um. I told her that she should have checked with me sooner.

THERAPIST: You had a conversation and you told her that she should have checked with you sooner?

JENNIFER: Yes. She didn't really say anything in response. It was a little awkward. I agreed to check to see when I could go. I started looking through my calendar and I got sidetracked with other things.

THERAPIST: Like what?

JENNIFER: Well, I just started thinking of all the things I had to do and then I went back and was looking through some of the information about my assignments that are coming up, I ended up spending a lot of time moving things around on my schedule and making lists of things I had to do.

THERAPIST: So, you got sidetracked by some details of your work and your schedule?

JENNIFER: Yes.

THERAPIST: Do you find that that your maladaptive pattern is coming up again, where you can get overly focused on certain details?

JENNIFER: Yes, I would agree with that. I spent a lot more time than I had to, just trying to get my schedule to be right. It was stressful.

THERAPIST: Right, like we discussed that pattern getting in the way of you completing tasks and doing the things you would like to do.

JENNIFER: Yes, and that makes me more frustrated and less motivated.

THERAPIST: The way you feel when you are depressed?

JENNIFER: (Pause) Yes, I guess that's true. It does seem to tie in together.

THERAPIST: You told your friend she should have asked you sooner and you got sidetracked in the details of your schedule. Did you do anything else in this situation?

JENNIFER: Yes, I just put her on hold. I sort of blew her off and said I was too busy to go this week. I just felt too overwhelmed. Maybe next week.

THERAPIST: Your third behavior was to put off going to the movies for another week. Is that right?

JENNIFER: Yes, that's right.

THERAPIST: Okay, Jennifer. What was it you wanted to get out of this situation? **(4)**

JENNIFER: I just wish she had given me more notice, so I could plan my schedule better.

THERAPIST: I agree, that might have been nice to have a little more notice, but I wonder if that is something you can control.

JENNIFER: No, I can't. That's what I think she should do but I can't control what she does.

THERAPIST: Then, what would be an outcome you would have liked that you do have control over?

JENNIFER: (Pause) I don't know. I guess I would have liked to go out with her. I would have liked to go to the movies and have a nice time.

THERAPIST: So, you would have wanted to go to the movies and have a fun time with your friend?

Commentary

Jennifer's initial desired outcome was not one she could control and is reflective of her maladaptive pattern. This is like the desired outcome she initially chose in the previous session. Both involved being critical and controlling of others. By redirecting her to a desired outcome that is within Jennifer's control, the therapist encouraged the shift to her adaptive pattern.

JENNIFER: Yes.

THERAPIST: So, what happened? **(5)**

JENNIFER: Well, I was annoyed. I sort of snapped at her over the phone and then I ended up not going.

THERAPIST: You felt annoyed and then reacted to your friend and decided not to go this week. Is that right?

JENNIFER: Yes, that's pretty much it.

THERAPIST: Then would you say you got the outcome you wanted? **(6)**

JENNIFER: No, definitely not.

THERAPIST: Okay, then would you like to review this situation again to see how it might have turned out differently for you, especially using your more adaptive pattern? **(7)**

JENNIFER: Yes, that sounds helpful.

THERAPIST: Good. Let's start with your thoughts. Your first thought was that your friend should have checked the schedule with you sooner. Did that thought help you or hurt you in getting what you wanted—which was to go to the movie with your friend? **(8)**

JENNIFER: I think it hurt me.

THERAPIST: How did it hurt you?

JENNIFER: Thinking that made me feel really annoyed and then that was all I could focus on.

THERAPIST: So, that thought caused you to only focus on one aspect of the situation?

JENNIFER: Yes. Just the negative part.

THERAPIST: What do you think would have been a more helpful thought in that situation?

JENNIFER: If I just thought it was nice of her to invite me. She could have invited anyone, and she asked me. That was nice.

THERAPIST: Alright, thinking that it was nice of her to invite you. How would that have been more helpful?

JENNIFER: I think it would have helped me be more grateful instead of critical.

THERAPIST: Do you often find yourself being more critical?

JENNIFER: (Pause) I guess you could say that. It's very frustrating when you can see that someone did something wrong or they just didn't put enough thought into it.

THERAPIST: I understand how that can be frustrating for you. How do you view that in terms of your pattern, as we discussed before?

JENNIFER: It can be hard to see the big picture sometimes. I think I do get focused on little things that other people don't focus on so much. And when I get focused on those things, it's hard to just get on with what I was doing.

THERAPIST: So, it gets in the way of what you want and need to do?

JENNIFER: Yes, I would say so. I never thought about it like that before, but it makes sense to me now.

THERAPIST: Let's move on to your second thought. Your thought was, "Doesn't she realize how busy I am?" Was that thought helpful or hurtful in getting your desired outcome of going to the movies?

JENNIFER: It did not help. It hurt because it was more criticism, like we said before.

THERAPIST: Then what would have been a more helpful thought for you in that moment?

JENNIFER: Probably realizing that she is busy, too. We have a class together so we both have the same amount of work, at least for that class.

THERAPIST: Good. How would thinking that she is busy too have helped you go to the movies?

JENNIFER: Well, then it would have made more sense to me that she waited a bit before asking me. I guess I don't know everything that she has going on. Everyone is very busy.

THERAPIST: Okay, then it would have helped you be more understanding?

JENNIFER: Yes, I think it would have.

THERAPIST: Good. Now your third thought was that your friend doesn't think before she does things. Did that thought help you or hurt you in getting what you wanted?

JENNIFER: That hurt me also. It's pretty much the same as the last two thoughts.

THERAPIST: How so?

JENNIFER: Well, it was critical of me. Then, all I could focus on was how agitated I felt and what she did wrong and thinking about what she should have done. There was no way I could go out and enjoy myself once I was in that mind-set.

THERAPIST: Okay, so you are finding that your maladaptive pattern influences your mood and then your behaviors.

JENNIFER: That really makes sense.

THERAPIST: What is a thought that would have been more helpful for your mind-set in that situation?

JENNIFER: Um, I guess that it was nice that she invited me. She couldn't choose the dates the certificate was valid for. She just wanted to go to the movies together.

THERAPIST: Right. Then how would that thought have helped you?

JENNIFER: It would have helped me focus on the good stuff and realize that she's not really at fault. It's not that she is bad at planning.

THERAPIST: It's sort of just the reality of the situation?

JENNIFER: Yes, right. It's not her fault.

THERAPIST: Good. Now let's move on to your behaviors. Your first behavior was that you told your friend she should have checked with you first. Did that behavior help you or hurt you to get to go to the movies? **(9)**

JENNIFER: Um, it was hurtful.

THERAPIST: How was it hurtful?

JENNIFER: I don't think she liked that. It didn't set a good tone. And it made me more upset. I wish I could have just let it go.

THERAPIST: So, you had difficulty letting it go. What do you think would have been a more helpful behavior?

JENNIFER: If I had just stayed calm and thanked her.

THERAPIST: Stayed calm. How would thanking her instead have helped?

JENNIFER: Well, I am very thankful so that would have been more accurate.

THERAPIST: It would have been more representative of how you feel?

JENNIFER: Yes. And it wouldn't be so harsh. It probably would have helped set a better mood, which would have inspired me to set a date to go to the movies.

THERAPIST: It would have helped you be more motivated to go and would have been more helpful for your relationship with your friend. Is that right?

JENNIFER: Yes, that really makes sense. I think it would have helped.

THERAPIST: Good. Your second behavior was that you got sidetracked looking at your schedule and all the things you must do. Did that help you or hurt you in getting what you wanted?

JENNIFER: It hurt, because it was just a bunch of time I spent being frustrated and getting upset. I felt sort of defeated after going through my schedule because it's like I don't have time for anything.

THERAPIST: So, doing that made you sidetracked and focused on what was going wrong instead of what was going well?

JENNIFER: Yes, that's true.

THERAPIST: I understand. If getting sidetracked led to you feeling frustrated and defeated, what do you think would have been a more helpful behavior in that situation?

JENNIFER: I still needed to look at my schedule, but if I would have just chosen a date that worked for me—a date I could go to the movies. I could have just chosen a date, put it in my schedule and that's it. No obsessing over it.

THERAPIST: I see. Then how would choosing a date and putting it in your schedule have helped you?

JENNIFER: It would have helped me just make the plans and move on to something else, instead of worrying about minor details.

THERAPIST: That makes sense, especially considering your maladaptive pattern.

JENNIFER: That's true. It's funny because I want to be organized but doing stuff like getting super focused on some pointless details makes me much less efficient. Plus, just scheduling something helps me because it gives me something to look forward to.

THERAPIST: That would reflect your adaptive pattern instead of your maladaptive one. Does that make sense?

JENNIFER: (Pause). Yeah. I can see that.

THERAPIST: How would it help you with your mood and motivation?

JENNIFER: It helps to have something fun to look forward to.

THERAPIST: So, making a decision without getting sidetracked with minor details can not only help you be more efficient, but also help you with your stress and your mood.

JENNIFER: Yes, I never thought about it that way before, but it makes sense now.

THERAPIST: I am glad that that makes sense for you. Your third behavior was to put off your friend and not go to the movies. Did that behavior help you or hurt you in getting what you wanted, which was to have a fun night at the movies with your friend?

JENNIFER: It hurt. It's just a result of everything else. The obsessing over details. And just my frustration and annoyance.

THERAPIST: So, at that point you were already annoyed and frustrated, largely from your focus on the details and criticism of your friend's actions.

JENNIFER: Yes, so at that point I was too frustrated to go.

THERAPIST: What would have been a more helpful behavior for you?

JENNIFER: If I had just made plans, like I said. Just choose a date that works for both of us and schedule that.

Commentary

Throughout the query sequence, Jennifer became less critical of others as she generated alterative thoughts and behaviors that were more aligned with her adaptive pattern. Her pattern shifting was evident, beginning with her review of her behavioral activation homework through the query sequence.

THERAPIST: Good. Now, on a scale from 0 to 10, where 0 is not at all and 10 is the most, how important is it for you to change your maladaptive pattern? **(10)**

JENNIFER: Um, I think it's a 9. I can see how some of the things I do affect my mood and get in the way of me doing what I want. Or doing things the way I want to. Be more efficient. Have more fun.

THERAPIST: That's good. It is good to hear it is very important to you. On the same scale, how confident are you that you can change this pattern?

JENNIFER: Um, I think a 7 today.

THERAPIST: Seven is more than halfway. What do you think it would take to move that to an 8 or even a 9?

JENNIFER: Um, I think if I can do my schedule this week without getting hyper-focused on the minor details.

THERAPIST: So, if you could put into action the things that we discussed today in regard to you planning to go to the movies?

JENNIFER: Yes. If I could plan to see the movie, that would be good. That would make me feel more confident. We can see it sometime this upcoming week. That would be good.

THERAPIST: Good. That gives you a chance to revisit this situation and perhaps employ some of the alternative thoughts and behaviors that you generated today in our session.

JENNIFER: Yes, that's true. Plus, I really want to go to the movie. And it's free because my friend has the gift certificate. So, that will be really nice.

THERAPIST: Often, it can help to role play these kinds of situations, so you can get some practice saying what you would like to say in the actual situation. Does that sound like something you would like to try here? **(Role play)**

JENNIFER: Sure.

THERAPIST: I can play the role of your friend. What is her name?

JENNIFER: Stephanie.

THERAPIST: Stephanie. Then you can just be yourself. Sound good?

JENNIFER: Sure.

THERAPIST: "Jennifer, I have those tickets to the movies and I want to use them before they expire. I know it's short notice, but the only available times are Thursday at 8:00 or Friday at 10:00. Can you go?"

JENNIFER: "I'd love to go. Let me just check my schedule and let you know when I can go." (Pause) I want to ask why she waited until last minute, but I don't think that's a good idea. I think I'll just check my schedule and choose a time and just go with that. So, I would say, "I can go Friday at 10."

THERAPIST: "Great. Friday works. I'll be there right on time, though. I'm busy with orchestra practice right before that so I'll be coming right at 10:00. I won't be late, but I can't get there early either. I hope that's okay."

JENNIFER: "Thanks for letting me know. I'll meet you out front at 10:00 on Friday."

THERAPIST: That was good. What did you think about the role play?

JENNIFER: It's funny because I would probably get annoyed that she was going to not come at least a few minutes early, so we can get good seats, but that's the time that works better for me and it was good that she told me, so I'm willing to compromise.

THERAPIST: You were willing to compromise in the role play.

JENNIFER: That's right. Now that I think about it, I can do that in real life.

Commentary

While Jennifer's motivation has improved greatly, her answer to the second MI question indicated she would benefit from an intervention tailored to improve her confidence. By scheduling a date with her friend and thereby resolving the situation analyzed during the query sequence, Jennifer will have the opportunity to practice her adaptive pattern in a real-world setting. Her success in this endeavor should increase her confidence in her ability to shift from a maladaptive to adaptive pattern. The role-play exercise provided Jennifer the opportunity to practice more adaptive and effective behaviors that will help her increase her social interest, thus decreasing her depression. The therapist's dialogue during the role play was intended to trigger her maladaptive pattern, but Jennifer was able to manage this unexpected aspect effectively. She then commented on the contrast between how she would normally react versus how she was able to react according to her change in pattern. Jennifer demonstrated increased confidence with her comment that she would be able to implement these behaviors in real life.

THERAPIST: Very good. I am glad we tried this exercise and I hope it will be helpful to you.

JENNIFER: Yes. Me too. I feel more confident about it now.

THERAPIST: There's another technique I would like to introduce you to. It is called reflecting "as if" and it can help you continue to visualize the ways in which you would like things to be different. Does that sound like something you would like to try? **(Reflecting "as if")**

JENNIFER: Sure. I'm not sure how that works but I would be willing to try it.

THERAPIST: Great. It isn't that difficult to do, and I think you will find it enjoyable. I would like you to imagine that all the changes you want to make in your life are already made and that things are as you would like them to be.

JENNIFER: Okay. I can do that.

THERAPIST: Can you describe what that would be like?

JENNIFER: Yes. I would be a lot less stressed out. I would be calm and feel good about myself. Maybe I would even be able to balance my work with my social life and feel less guilty about everything.

THERAPIST: Very good. Can you describe what your typical day would be like if things were as you would like them to be?

JENNIFER: Yes. I would wake up on time and feel excited about the day and refreshed instead of tired. I would take a run or go to the gym and then shower and have a healthy breakfast. Then maybe I would meet some friends for coffee before class. In class, I would be excited about what I was learning instead of thinking about everything I have to do and being stressed out. Then after class I would stick to my schedule and get my work done as I had planned. And, if I didn't finish something or things didn't work out the way I wanted them to, I would feel okay about it. I would say something to myself like, "It's okay; you did your best and you're going to continue to do well." Then, after that I would maybe meet some friends at a yoga class or go out for some drinks depending on what day it was. I would make plans down the line for stuff, like maybe taking a weekend road trip with friends or visiting my family. I would be able to talk to my parents on the phone and not get upset or feel guilty. I would be able to enjoy myself and not criticize myself so much. That's probably it.

THERAPIST: That sounds very nice! It captures your goals of wanting to feel more motivated, improve your mood, and balance your work with your social life.

JENNIFER: That would be great!

THERAPIST: I agree with you. What do you think of the reflecting "as if" exercise?

JENNIFER: I liked it. Maybe I'll do it by myself when I'm feeling overwhelmed.

THERAPIST: I think that's a great idea. We are getting close to the end of our session, so why don't we schedule some more activities for you to complete this upcoming week?

JENNIFER: Yes, that sounds good.

THERAPIST: Let's schedule three activities for you this coming week. Let's have two of them be pleasurable activities and one be an activity that you must do.

JENNIFER: Well, I have been enjoying walking more. It's nice because it's not like sports practice. There's no goal; I don't have to push myself.

THERAPIST: That's different for you.

JENNIFER: Yes, it is. I can just enjoy myself instead of having to work toward something. It's nice.

THERAPIST: So, you have enjoyed slowing down and maybe taking some time to enjoy the present moment.

JENNIFER: Yes.

THERAPIST: Which day would you like to complete that activity?

JENNIFER: I was hoping to do it on Thursday after class.

THERAPIST: Thursday you can take a walk for about 20 minutes. Where will you be taking the walk?

JENNIFER: I will just go around my apartment and walk around the neighborhood.

THERAPIST: That's good. Do you have a backup for that activity?

JENNIFER: Yes, I can probably go to the gym. I like the elliptical machine.

THERAPIST: That sounds like a good workout. What is a second activity you can schedule?

JENNIFER: Um, there's an improv show on campus on Saturday evening. The posters for that looked quite funny. I'd like to go, and I know a few people who will be there.

THERAPIST: It looks entertaining and fun to you and it will give you the opportunity to see your friends.

JENNIFER: Yes. It's an hour-long show. So, I can do that on Saturday.

THERAPIST: Great. Finally, what is an activity that is something you have to do?

JENNIFER: Oh, I have a big research paper coming up. I need to go to the library and get help finding books and articles. I need to make an appointment to meet with a librarian. They offer half-hour appointments where they help you search for the resources.

THERAPIST: That sounds very helpful and a good way to help you get started and find the correct resources. Have you scheduled that yet?

JENNIFER: No, but I would like to go on Friday. You can schedule online. I can do it when I get home today.

THERAPIST: Then, your third activity will be to go have a meeting with the librarian to find the resources you need for your research paper. You would like to go on Friday and today you will schedule that appointment online.

JENNIFER: Yes, that's what I'm going to do.

THERAPIST: If you cannot make it on Friday, is there another day you can go to the library?

JENNIFER: Yes, I can do it either Thursday or Saturday. Any one of those days works.

THERAPIST: Great. And I'll have you continue to keep track of those activities using your log and rate your level of completion and enjoyment for each of those activities on the scale from 0 to 10.

JENNIFER: Okay, I will.

THERAPIST: I would also like you to continue filling out your mood chart as you have been.

JENNIFER: Sure, I'll continue with that.

THERAPIST: So just one more thing. Please fill out the SRS form so we can see if you have been getting what you want out of our sessions. **(SRS review)**

JENNIFER: Alright.

THERAPIST: I see you were satisfied with our session today and we covered what you wanted to talk about.

JENNIFER: I really wanted to talk about my social stuff, like what happened with my friend and how frustrated I felt. I feel better about it now.

THERAPIST: Very good. I look forward to meeting with you next time.

Commentary

Jennifer's agreeableness to the behavioral activation intervention, and willingness to schedule more activities of varied levels of difficulty, indicates her motivation, energy, and pleasure derived from activities is increasing. This was also reflected in her Mood Scale rating, PHQ-9 score, and ORS score. Her high SRS score likely suggests that her pattern was not triggered in this session, despite several challenges. Additionally, although Jennifer is a very agreeable client, she was still slow to warm. Her SRS scores were 38 in sessions two and three. The score of 40 in this session is more indicative of a therapeutic alliance marked by trust. Finally, Jennifer is shifting from her maladaptive pattern to a more adaptive one, as evidenced by her improved mood and increased social interest. It is expected that her score on the SII-SF during session five will indicate this change.

Concluding Note

In session four, the reflecting "as if" intervention is used to help the client visualize how life would be different if the changes the client would like to see were already made. This helps the client replace current ways of thinking with more adaptive ones. The query sequence is used to continue to facilitate pattern change. In the exemplar case, Jennifer is redirected to a desired outcome that is within her control, so she can generate adaptive, replacement thoughts and behaviors that will help her achieve the outcomes she wants. Finally, role playing is used to help the client practice new skills reflective of the adaptive pattern. This process also helps build the client's confidence so that she can shift to a more adaptive pattern.

References

Carich, M. (1997). Variations of the "as if" technique. In J. Carlson. & S. Slavik, (Eds.). (1997). *Techniques in Adlerian psychology*. (pp. 153–160). Washington DC: Accelerated Development. Corsini, R. (1966). *Role playing in psychotherapy: A manual*. Chicago, IL: Aldine.

La Guardia, A. C., Watts, R. E., & Garza, Y. (2013). A framework for applying reflecting "as if" with nonsuicidal self-injurious clients. *Journal of Individual Psychology, 69*(3), 20–222.

Watts, R. E. (2003). Reflecting "as if": An integrative process in couples counseling. *The Family Journal, 11*(1), 73–75.

Watts, R. E., & Garza, Y. (2008). Using children's drawings to facilitate the acting "as if" technique. *Journal of Individual Psychology, 64*(1), 113–118.

Watts, R. E., & Trusty, J. (2003). Using imaginary team members in reflecting "as if". *Journal of Constructivist Psychology, 16*(4), 335–340.

8

The Middle Phase of Therapy

Learning Objectives

In this chapter, you will learn the following:

1. The push button technique
2. How to continue to focus sessions on pattern change
3. How to continue assessing change in symptoms, pattern, and social interest
4. How to make critical therapeutic decisions
5. A continuing case of how Adlerian pattern-focused therapy is practiced

This chapter analyzes the middle phase of Jennifer's therapy: sessions five, six, seven, and eight. These sessions are dedicated to continuing symptom reduction, pattern shifting, and increasing social interest. The Social Interest Inventory-Short Form (SII-SF) is administered again in the fifth session as part of progress monitoring. In session five, Jennifer reports the ability to catch herself acting according to her old pattern and replace thoughts and behaviors without the assistance of the therapist. The therapist demonstrates effective therapeutic decision making and intervention implementation. Change continues in sessions six and seven, with Jennifer's increasing ability to recognize and manage her pattern triggers. The therapist introduces the push button technique in session eight, giving Jennifer another means to control her emotional states. At this session, Jennifer's depression symptoms drop to a sub-clinical level, indicating achievement of first order goals. This chapter presents transcription selections from sessions five, six, seven, and eight of the case of Jennifer, with commentary.

Push Button Technique

The push button technique (Mosak, 1985; Mosak & Maniacci, 1998) was developed as an Adlerian intervention for depression. This technique allows individuals to take control of their emotional experiences by "pushing a button" to replace negative feeling states with more positive ones. The individual replaces feeling states without engaging in cognitive restructuring, interpretation, or exposure. To implement this technique, the client is first introduced to the intervention and explained its purpose. To demonstrate it, the therapist asks the client to close his or her eyes and concentrate on an unpleasant memory while describing the feelings associated with it. The client is then asked to concentrate on a pleasant memory and describe its associated feelings. Then, the therapist instructs the client to visualize pushing a button while switching back and forth between feeling states and instructs the client to practice the technique outside of session and generate more positive memories to use when pushing the button. The technique is demonstrated in the excerpt from session eight, found later in this chapter.

Case of Jennifer—Session 5 Transcription

Jennifer completed the Social Interest Inventory-Short Form (SII-SF) immediately prior to this session, along with the other standardized instruments. Her SII-SF score indicates a marked increase in social interest, 12 points higher than her score at the intake session. It is consistent with her PHQ-9 score dropping into the mild depression range, as well as her improved ORS score. Jennifer begins implementing alternative thoughts and behaviors outside of session. In session five, she identifies some triggers to her pattern and demonstrates the ability to overcome several triggers without the assistance of the therapist. Select sections from this transcription are presented next.

TABLE 8.1 Session 5 Assessment Scores

Patient Health Questionnaire-9 (PHQ-9)	8 (mild depression)
Outcome Rating Scale (ORS)	27 total: 6 individually, 7 interpersonally, 7 socially, 7 overall
Session Rating Scale (SRS)	40
Mood Scale	7
Social Interest Inventory-Short Form (SII-SF)	33
MI scores	Importance: 9 Confidence: 6

THERAPIST: Okay, let's move on to reviewing your ORS form for today. **(ORS review)**

JENNIFER: That sounds fine.

THERAPIST: Can you tell me more about your rating on individual functioning?

JENNIFER: Sure. Yes, I felt really frustrated a lot of times this week. But, I felt like I was able to manage it better than usual. So that was pretty good.

THERAPIST: Okay, I understand you had some frustrations, but I am glad to hear that you were able to manage some of these feelings. What helped you manage that situation better?

JENNIFER: Um, I thought about some of the things we talked about in here and I was able to think, "Okay, what am I thinking in this moment?" And I was able to think that it's not the end of the world that I felt overwhelmed by my work. You know? I can break tasks down and manage them.

THERAPIST: Okay, so identifying that your pattern of being perfectionistic and sometimes critical was coming up and then evaluating your thoughts and alternatives helped you?

JENNIFER: Yes, that's very cool that I was able to apply that.

Commentary

Jennifer reported that she was able to catch herself thinking and behaving in ways reflective of her maladaptive pattern. She then applied alternative thoughts and behaviors on her own, outside of the session. This behavior indicates Jennifer's move toward third order change. This suggests that she can continue to respond—on her own—in adaptive ways when she has completed therapy. The therapist tied Jennifer's behavior back to her pattern. This exchange was validating for Jennifer and likely increased her level of confidence that she could change her maladaptive pattern.

JENNIFER: Yes, socially, things went well with my friends at the show. But what brought my rating down a little was that interaction with my parents. They were annoyed that I said I would call but I forgot it was the same day as the show. I called them the next day, but they were upset because they waited for me to call.

THERAPIST: And how was that resolved?

JENNIFER: I don't know if it was really resolved. It was more like we started talking about other things and didn't mention it again.

THERAPIST: So, you had a good time with your friends and then some tension with your parents that was not really addressed but you have moved past it?

JENNIFER: Yes. I don't think they're going to bring up that incident again. Maybe if it happened again, they would.

THERAPIST: How would you rate yourself on the mood scale?

JENNIFER: I would say feeling a little better. About a 7 on the mood scale. I was really stressed this week because of a group project.

Commentary

Though Jennifer discussed this incident involving her parents, the therapist decided not to further process the dynamic with Jennifer's parents at this time. Despite her family's influence on her maladaptive pattern, this interaction with her parents did not appear to trigger Jennifer's pattern, suggesting an improvement in her functioning. She indicated that she was not too distressed over her parents' behavior and still reported a relatively high mood scale score for the week as well as an increased social interest score. Jennifer's ability to manage this stressful interaction with her parents reflects her move toward a more adaptive pattern. If Jennifer was more distressed about the interaction, or if she were to bring it up again in future sessions, it would warrant more attention from the therapist. Otherwise, spending more time discussing it might be an unnecessary distraction from the course of therapy. Situations like this can be challenging therapeutic decisions for therapists.

THERAPIST: Good. Now, let's move on to your behaviors. Your first behavior was to complete portions of the other students' assignments. Did that behavior help you or hurt you focus on your own work? **(9)**

JENNIFER: Um, it was hurtful. It took up all my time and I got hyper-focused on it.

THERAPIST: Okay, so you noticed some of your pattern again, the excess focus on details?

JENNIFER: Yes, it comes up most in situations like this is where something depends on other people being competent.

THERAPIST: Sometimes you find yourself getting critical because of this pattern?

JENNIFER: Yes, I would say that. I do get critical.

THERAPIST: What tends to happen when you get critical of others?

JENNIFER: Well, it just leaves me upset. And then I focus on tiny things and get more annoyed. It's like a cycle.

THERAPIST: So, you notice the pattern perpetuates itself in a way.

JENNIFER: Yes, it does.

THERAPIST: Okay, then in this situation, what do you think would have been a more helpful behavior?

JENNIFER: If I had just done my own work, just my own part. I really needed that time and I actually spent it doing another people's work. If I had just done my work, it's really respecting my own time more and then I would have had the time I wanted for myself.

THERAPIST: Just focusing on your own work would have left you the spare time you needed and would have been more respectful of your time and your schedule.

JENNIFER: Yes. I don't often think about the fact that my time is worth something. This has helped me realize I need to prioritize.

THERAPIST: Okay, good. So, you are realizing that prioritizing your time in a way that is respectful of what you need will be helpful to you.

JENNIFER: Yes.

Commentary

While analyzing her behaviors during the query sequence, Jennifer connected her perfectionistic pattern to her tendency to criticize others and recognized the self-perpetuating nature of her pattern. This is a major indicator of change for Jennifer. Her shift toward a more adaptive pattern helped Jennifer become more aware of her maladaptive pattern's effect on her relationships, and her increased level of social interest bolstered her motivation to change this pattern so she could foster better relationships. Finally, in session five, Jennifer recognized specific triggers to her pattern, which will be useful in future relapse prevention planning.

Case of Jennifer—Session 6 Transcription

Change accomplished in session five carries over into session six. Jennifer presents a situation, while reviewing her behavioral activation activities, in which she managed to stay on task and not be sidetracked by minor details and setbacks. This change is reflected in her score on the PHQ-9, ORS, and Mood Scale. Additionally, Jennifer's confidence in her ability to change her maladaptive pattern increases. Select sections from this transcription are presented next.

TABLE 8.2 Session 6 Assessment Scores

Patient Health Questionnaire-9 (PHQ-9)	7 (mild depression)
Outcome Rating Scale (ORS)	30 total: 8 individually, 7 interpersonally, 7 socially, 8 overall
Session Rating Scale (SRS)	40
Mood Scale	7
MI Scores	Importance: 9 Confidence: 7

THERAPIST: (Pause) I see your first activity was to go to a yoga class on campus. How did you rate that activity?

JENNIFER: I rated it a 9 for completion and 7 for enjoyment. It was a nice class, but I couldn't get some of the poses right. That's why I rated it a 9 for completion. I don't really consider it that I completed the whole class because I really didn't complete the poses.

THERAPIST: I see. So, you completed the class but did not give yourself a 10 for completion because you did not perfect the poses. Is that correct?

JENNIFER: Yes, well when you say it that way, it seems a little silly. I can't really get them perfect.

THERAPIST: So, do you see that as possibly being part of your perfectionistic pattern that we identified?

JENNIFER: (Pause) Yes. Now that I think about it, it's frustrating and kind of silly that I don't cut myself any slack.

THERAPIST: Right. You also are not rewarding yourself as much as you could be for what you accomplished.

JENNIFER: That's true, too.

JENNIFER: It was fun, and I saw some friends there. I felt great when I was done, and it led to me eating healthy the rest of the day. It's really motivating.

THERAPIST: Yes, it can be. Was there anything else that was good about this activity?

JENNIFER: Well, now that we kind of talked about my self-criticism, I can look at it a little differently. I didn't perfect the poses, but I learned a lot of poses and got further than I thought I could. So that was good.

Commentary

Jennifer's pattern was triggered by her behavioral activation activity when she could not perform the yoga poses to perfection. Despite her increased insight into her pattern, the maladaptive pattern was operative in this situation, leading to Jennifer's frustration. The therapist helped Jennifer connect the dots in this situation and Jennifer realized her self-criticism is not only unwarranted but also reinforces her pattern and affects her mood. Some pattern shift occurred in this interaction as evidenced in Jennifer's appraisal of the activity.

THERAPIST: That's great. (Pause) What was not as good about this activity?

JENNIFER: Now that we're talking about it, I don't think there was anything that was really not good about it. I'm really glad I went, and I think I'm going to do it again when it comes up. It's nice that it was free.

THERAPIST: That certainly helps. (Pause) Your second activity was one you had to do, which was go to the study group. How did you rate that activity?

JENNIFER: I rated it 10 for completion and 6 for enjoyment. It wasn't really a fun activity.

THERAPIST: I understand. It was more of something you had to do, which is what we were going for when we scheduled the activities. A balance between fun activities and necessary activities. So, I know this wasn't a fun one, but what was good about this activity?

JENNIFER: I did get a lot out of it. There were some homework sections and questions I was really struggling with and I got a lot of help with those. I was able to figure out what I needed. I was also able to resist taking charge of other people's work for them.

THERAPIST: That's great. So, that's more of what we were addressing with your pattern. How did you resist that and focus on your own work?

JENNIFER: Um, I just told myself that their work really doesn't affect me and that I'll have more time to myself and more time to relax if I just focus on my own work and prioritize.

THERAPIST: Great. That is what we talked about in our previous session. Were you able to incorporate some of the alternative thoughts and behaviors that you identified then?

JENNIFER: Yes, I was. It was a good feeling when I realized that I could just let certain things go and not get too focused on them. I felt relieved.

THERAPIST: That's wonderful! I am glad you have been getting so much out of our sessions together and that you found the strategies you learned to be useful.

JENNIFER: Yes. It's amazing how much more time and energy I have when I can prioritize and manage my time better.

THERAPIST: That's great. Now, what was not so good about the study group activity?

JENNIFER: Um, it was just kind of boring. It was a drag. The work is very intense, and I felt tired afterwards. It wasn't bad, just not very fun.

THERAPIST: Then, you got what you needed from it, and you didn't overextend yourself, but it just wasn't a very fun activity.

JENNIFER: That's right.

THERAPIST: Okay, now your third activity was to prepare some food, particularly some fruits and vegetables for smoothies. How did that go?

JENNIFER: I rated that an 8 for completion and an 8 for enjoyment. I realized I didn't have one ingredient I needed, and I didn't want to go out and get it so I just made them without it.

THERAPIST: All right, so you were able to continue making them even though you were missing one ingredient?

JENNIFER: Yeah, I guess I usually wouldn't do that.

THERAPIST: What was good about this activity?

JENNIFER: Well, I was glad that I was able to continue even though I didn't have one ingredient. Normally, I would obsess over that and stop everything. I just wanted to add some frozen blueberries and I didn't have any and I just thought, "These aren't essential." So, I made my recipes anyway. I was pleased with that.

THERAPIST: So, you are pleased with these changes you have been seeing in yourself?

JENNIFER: Yes, I am. It was also fun to be able to make the recipes that I had been wanting to try and to feel more prepared. So now I have these frozen smoothies and I can just blend one at a time when I'm on the go.

THERAPIST: That sounds great. A really good idea, too.

JENNIFER: I think so.

THERAPIST: What was not as good about this activity?

JENNIFER: Um, probably just that I was missing an ingredient. I also spilled some yogurt on my counter and it went in between the counter and the stove.

THERAPIST: That sounds frustrating.

JENNIFER: It was, but I managed it. I managed to clean it up. So that was fine. Nothing else was bad about the activity. I think I'm going to do it again.

THERAPIST: Good. I am glad to hear that you have found some things to be easier and less irritating to you, now that you are using some of these alternatives on an increasingly regular basis.

JENNIFER: Yes, I definitely am.

Commentary

Jennifer completed her assigned activities, indicating that although her pattern was triggered in a few instances, she has achieved enough first and second order change to successfully mitigate these challenges. She employed alternative thoughts and behaviors consistently, as she was able to catch herself slipping back into the maladaptive pattern, indicating third order change. The therapist will continue to build on this success in future sessions before helping Jennifer make a relapse prevention plan.

Case of Jennifer – Session 7 Transcription

In session seven, Jennifer's symptoms continue to improve, her social interest increases, and her pattern continues to shift to one that is more adaptive. Jennifer improves her ability to manage obstacles and finds her pattern is triggered less often. As a result of her improvements, both her ratings for importance and confidence increase from session six. Select sections from this transcription are presented next.

TABLE 8.3 Session 7 Assessment Scores

Patient Health Questionnaire-9 (PHQ-9)	6 (mild depression)
Outcome Rating Scale (ORS)	31 total: 7 individually, 8 interpersonally, 8 socially, 8 overall
Session Rating Scale (SRS)	40
Mood Scale	7
MI scores	Importance: 10 Confidence: 8

THERAPIST: Let's look at your mood chart from this past week. **(mood chart review)**

JENNIFER: Sure. I wrote excited and pleasant more than I wrote irritated and frustrated this week. Also, I was less tired overall.

THERAPIST: I can see that. It is good to see your overall moods improving.

JENNIFER: Yes, it's nice to be able to track it in this way.

THERAPIST: I'm glad this has been useful for you. Why don't we now review your activities from last week?

JENNIFER: Okay, I had a pretty good week, so we can discuss that.

THERAPIST: That's good. I look forward to hearing about it. Your first activity was one that you had to do—your assignment. How did you rate that activity?

JENNIFER: I rated it an 8 for completion and 5 for enjoyment. I was very pleased that I worked on the assignment during the time I scheduled. That was an achievement for me.

THERAPIST: Right, I remember the situation we discussed last week when you struggled to stick to your schedule.

JENNIFER: Yes, this time it was a lot better. I couldn't finish the assignment during the time that I allotted. It ended up taking longer than I thought it would and I had to come back to it another time. That's why I didn't give it a 10 for completion. But I was happy that I was able to work on it when I wanted to. I felt a lot more efficient.

THERAPIST: What would you say helped you to achieve this goal this week?

JENNIFER: Um, thinking of some of the alternative thoughts that we've discussed. It was helpful to go over that last situation with you. This time I thought, okay, if I don't do my assignment now then I'll have to cancel another activity, and I didn't want to do that. Then I reminded myself that what I needed to do didn't have to be perfect. I can always edit my assignment after it's done. I must just get something written.

THERAPIST: Very good. So, you used some alternative thoughts to remind yourself of your priorities and that what you do doesn't have to be perfect, so you didn't stop yourself before you even got started.

JENNIFER: Yes, exactly.

THERAPIST: Okay, that's wonderful! (Pause) So, what would you say was good about this activity?

JENNIFER: I felt great about being able to work on it when I said that I would. And even though I didn't finish in that time frame, I got most of it done, which was a big relief.

THERAPIST: That's great. Now, what was not as good about this activity?

JENNIFER: Honestly, it was kind of boring. It was very tedious to find articles and have to read through research materials I didn't need. I was a little annoyed that it had to drag out and required me to work on it longer than I had hoped, but that wasn't that bad.

THERAPIST: How frustrated were you by this assignment compared to previous ones?

JENNIFER: Not as frustrated. I was able to remain calm and just deal with the fact that I didn't finish when I wanted to. It wasn't the end of the world.

THERAPIST: Very good. So, you are finding that you don't feel as irritated as you did before and you're learning to temper your striving for perfection.

JENNIFER: Yes, because it never actually gets me what I want and so I end up just feeling bad for nothing.

THERAPIST: It's an exercise in futility.

JENNIFER: That's right.

Commentary

Despite some obstacles, Jennifer successfully completed her behavioral activation homework. Through the activity, she was able to reframe several of her thoughts to reflect her more adaptive pattern and gained further understanding of how her perfectionistic pattern affects different areas of her life.

THERAPIST: Good. Now, your third activity was to take another walk. How did that go?

JENNIFER: I rated that 8 for completion and 8 for enjoyment. It looked like it was about to rain so I had to turn around and go back. Luckily, I got home in time before it started raining.

THERAPIST: Okay, so you couldn't really complete the activity because of the weather.

JENNIFER: Yes. Otherwise it was good.

THERAPIST: What was good about this activity?

JENNIFER: It was great to be outside in a relaxing setting. I often do things sort of all or nothing. I'm realizing that now. Like, I normally wouldn't go out and take a walk just because it's relaxing or pleasant. It has to be about me competing in a sport or preparing for a competition.

THERAPIST: I see. So, you are realizing that in the past you thought you could only go out and get some exercise and some fresh air if it was related to sports or a competition or something you had to do. But now, you are seeing that relaxation and leisure can be just as important.

JENNIFER: That's right. I can't believe I just never explored that before. It was like anything that I wasn't doing on purpose for a competition wasn't worth doing. It seems very silly now because when I go out on these walks, I feel good and I get to enjoy some quiet time and some nature. It helps me slow down.

THERAPIST: Yes. So, now you are doing it on purpose but for reasons other than sports or competition.

JENNIFER: Yes, I'm doing it to relax. And to stay healthy and active.

THERAPIST: Okay, that's great. You are finding that your health and your enjoyment are just as important to you as training for a sport.

JENNIFER: Yes, it's true.

THERAPIST: Okay, good. Now, what was not so good about this activity?

JENNIFER: Like I said, it started raining. Or, I could tell it was about to rain. Luckily, I didn't get caught in it, but I did have to turn around and I couldn't go as far or as long as I had planned. That was so disappointing.

THERAPIST: Right. Now, you are finding yourself disappointed if you cannot finish an activity, whereas when you first came in, you found it difficult to get going or do any pleasurable things.

JENNIFER: Yes, that's true. I didn't think about that. I guess doing those first activities we planned, when it was hard for me to get motivated, has really helped me get motivated to do more things. I'm also enjoying these activities more. Now that we are talking about it, I realize I haven't felt like I am dragging as much, and things have been easier and a lot more fun.

THERAPIST: I'm so glad to hear that. I'm glad that this exercise has been so useful to you, and that you are feeling more motivated and enjoying yourself more.

JENNIFER: Yes, I really have been.

THERAPIST: Okay, good. Now, let's move on to reviewing your ORS form for today. **(ORS review)**

JENNIFER: Okay.

THERAPIST: Can you tell me more about your rating for how you have been doing individually?

JENNIFER: Yes, it's been good. Like I said, I'm more motivated. My mood is better. I've been getting things done and finding time to enjoy myself. I feel more accomplished.

THERAPIST: Okay good. So, as we discussed, you have been feeling more motivated. You've been enjoying yourself more and you notice an increase in your mood.

JENNIFER: Yes, and like I said, I'm learning that everything doesn't have to have a purpose, like for school. I can just do things because I like to or because they make me feel good.

THERAPIST: Good. Can you tell me more about your rating for the interpersonal category?

JENNIFER: Yes, that was much better this week than the last. A couple of weeks ago, before our last session, I was having a hard time getting out. I was so busy, I didn't really connect with a lot of people. This week was much better. I talked to my best friend on the phone, too, and we caught up about a lot of things. That was quite good, and I appreciated it. She called me yesterday and I was able to make some time to chat.

THERAPIST: Okay, great. How about socially?

JENNIFER: I was able to be social this week and it went well. School has also been going better, especially now that I'm learning to prioritize and allowing myself to do things somewhat less than perfect.

THERAPIST: Wonderful! So, you're finding that letting yourself do things that aren't perfect allows you to get a lot more done, prioritize, and have more fun?

JENNIFER: Yes, that's true. It's a big weight off my shoulders.

THERAPIST: Great, and how about your overall rating?

JENNIFER: My overall rating was good. I'm just feeling better knowing that I can relax a little, and I can enjoy my time here at school instead of just freaking out about my grades and my work and getting irritated whenever things interrupt me.

THERAPIST: Okay, so your ratings have improved because you are finding yourself enjoying your experience at school more, rather than everything being a chore.

JENNIFER: That's right.

THERAPIST: Good, and how would you rate yourself on the mood scale?

JENNIFER: I would say 7 on the mood scale. There were some ups and downs, but I can really tell how much better I have been feeling and how much my mood and my motivation has improved.

THERAPIST: Good. It's very good to hear that your mood has been improving and that you have found that dealing with your perfectionistic pattern can help you feel better and be more motivated.

Commentary

This portion of the session reflects change on three levels: symptom reduction, pattern shifting, and increasing social interest. Jennifer initiated much of the talk about change in the interaction with the therapist and successfully navigated several obstacles during the past week.

TABLE 8.4 Session 8 Assessment Scores

Patient Health Questionnaire-9 (PHQ-9)	5 (minimal to no depression)
Outcome Rating Scale (ORS)	32 total: 9 individually, 7 interpersonally, 8 socially, 8 overall
Session Rating Scale (SRS)	40
Mood Scale	8
MI scores	Importance: 10
	Confidence: 8

Case of Jennifer—Session 8 Transcription

Jennifer's PHQ-9 score now drops below the clinical threshold, indicating minimal to no depression. Her Mood Scale score reflects this change as well. Jennifer's ORS scores reflect continued symptom improvement and increasing social interest. The push button technique is introduced. Select sections from this transcription are presented nex.

THERAPIST:	Let's start by looking over your thoughts. Your first thought was, "I'm going to fail the test." Did that thought help you or hurt you in getting what you wanted, which was to balance studying and get some sleep? **(8)**
JENNIFER:	That was hurtful.
THERAPIST:	It was hurtful?
JENNIFER:	Yes.
THERAPIST:	How was it hurtful?
JENNIFER:	It made me feel overwhelmed and made it more difficult to concentrate.
THERAPIST:	It made it more difficult to concentrate because you felt overwhelmed?
JENNIFER:	Yes.
THERAPIST:	I can see how that must have been difficult. What do you think would have been a more helpful thought in that instance?
JENNIFER:	If I thought that I'm doing well in the class, so I probably know more than I'm giving myself credit for.
THERAPIST:	Okay, so you're probably not giving yourself enough credit?
JENNIFER:	Yes, that's right. I've been getting good grades in the class so far.
THERAPIST:	Do you think that is something that comes up somewhat regularly, not giving yourself enough credit?
JENNIFER:	Yeah, it really does. I do that a lot. It's pretty upsetting.
THERAPIST:	Yes, I remember you mentioning that before. How do you see your pattern playing into that?
JENNIFER:	I think that constantly telling myself I must be perfect or that I have to get everything to be a specific way. I just ignore the things I do well. I only focus on the stuff I think I'm not doing well enough.
THERAPIST:	And what do you think of your estimation of the things you are not doing well enough. Do you think your self-evaluation is fair?
JENNIFER:	No, I now see that it is not. I hold myself to an overly high standard, so I'm too critical about a lot of things that I do.
THERAPIST:	So, your expectations are unrealistic, you criticize yourself too harshly, and ignore the things you do well?

JENNIFER: Yes. That really takes a toll on my mood.

THERAPIST: It sounds like you're seeing that pattern of conscientiousness to the point of ineffectiveness tied into your depressed mood again. Being a cause of it?

JENNIFER: Yes, I really think so. I usually only feel bad when I am in that mind-set.

THERAPIST: Okay. How would the replacement thought that you are doing well in the class and maybe not giving yourself enough credit, how would that thought have helped you get what you wanted?

JENNIFER: I think it would have helped me feel more confident. And maybe I would have let myself get some sleep if I felt like I was going to do well.

Commentary

In this exchange, the therapist helped Jennifer both restructure and replace some of her maladaptive thoughts. Here, Jennifer's pattern of realistic conscientiousness proved helpful. Jennifer cares about doing things the right way, so the more she understands how her maladaptive pattern hinders her, the more motivated she is to replace her thoughts and behaviors with those indicative of a more adaptive pattern.

JENNIFER: It's going to be important for me to practice the strategies we talked about. Like scheduling a time to stop working.

THERAPIST: I agree that will make a huge difference. It seems like you can feel calm and confident at times, but sometimes it can be difficult to balance that with feeling stressed and overwhelmed.

JENNIFER: Yes, it can be very difficult sometimes. It seems so easy to slide back into some of those behaviors that make me depressed.

THERAPIST: Of course, that is understandable. Especially when you are still learning and practicing those new behaviors. I would like to introduce you to another technique. This is called the push button technique and is meant to help you bring about more pleasant moods instead of negative ones. How does that sound to you?

JENNIFER: I think I would like to try that. I would like to have more pleasant moods instead of negative ones.

THERAPIST: Okay, so if it's okay with you, I want you to start by thinking of something that makes you feel that negative mood. Something that makes you feel sad.

JENNIFER: Okay. Okay, I'm thinking of something.

THERAPIST: What are you thinking of?

JENNIFER: I'm thinking about when my grandmother died. She had Alzheimer's. That makes me feel sad.

THERAPIST: How sad are you about that thought on a Mood Scale from 0 to 10, where 1 is the saddest?

JENNIFER: Probably a 1 or a 2. We were close when I was little.

THERAPIST: That must have been a difficult loss for you.

JENNIFER: It really was.

THERAPIST: I am sorry to hear that. We can move away from that thought now. I would like you to think of something that makes you feel happy. A place, a good memory, something that puts you in a good mood.

JENNIFER: I'm thinking about my last birthday party. It was a great time with all my friends. We all got dressed up and went out. That was a fun day and I felt really relaxed.

THERAPIST: How do you feel thinking about it now?

JENNIFER: I feel relaxed now. I feel happy thinking about it and it makes me want to plan another fun night with my friends.

THERAPIST: Okay, so you feel more motivated and in a happier mood thinking about that memory?

JENNIFER: Yes.

THERAPIST: And how sad or distressed do you feel now, on a scale from 0 to 10?

JENNIFER: Oh, I would say 2 while I'm thinking about that memory.

THERAPIST: So, that is a big difference between the first sad memory and this happy memory?

JENNIFER: Yes, it really is a big difference.

THERAPIST: Do you see how you can bring about two entirely different moods by thinking of either a negative or positive memory?

JENNIFER: Yes, I would like to have more moods like when I was thinking about the happy thought.

THERAPIST: Now, I want you to think of another sad thing and this time I want you to imagine two buttons that you can push. It can be like a round, black button, something you can imagine yourself pushing. Can you picture that? **(push button technique)**

JENNIFER: Yes, I can see it.

THERAPIST: Good. Now I want you to imagine pressing that button when you think of this sad thought. Do you have a thought in mind?

JENNIFER: Yes. I am thinking about when my close friend in high school had to move away. Her mom got a job in another state and she left in the middle of the school year. That was very hard for me because we were in all our classes and some clubs together. It was weird having to go back to school after she moved, and everything seemed different.

THERAPIST: That sounds like a very difficult experience, having to carry on without your best friend.

JENNIFER: Yeah, it was. I feel sad just thinking about it.

THERAPIST: Okay, now I want you to imagine a second button, but this is the one you push when you want to be in a happy mood.

JENNIFER: Okay.

THERAPIST: I would like you to imagine that button while thinking of a happy thought.

JENNIFER: Yeah.

THERAPIST: Do you have a thought in mind?

JENNIFER: Um, yes. I'm thinking about after graduation, when my friends and I spent a weekend at the beach. One of my friend's parents has a house at the beach and they let us stay there for the weekend as sort of a graduation present. It was so relaxing. We had no responsibilities, nothing to worry about. We could stay up all night without having to stress about anything.

THERAPIST: That sounds like a wonderful memory with your friends.

JENNIFER: Yes.

THERAPIST: How do you feel thinking about that?

JENNIFER: I feel good! I feel happy thinking about those things. A lot less stressed than when I think about my work or some of those sad memories.

THERAPIST: Better than when you are being hard on yourself with your assignments?

JENNIFER: Oh, yes. Completely different than when I'm upset over what I did or didn't do on an assignment.

THERAPIST: I would like you to think of more things that bring on those good feelings. They could be memories, places, or things. Practice thinking of those things while thinking about pushing the button that makes you feel happy. And when you find yourself feeling stressed or having a low mood, I would like you to push that button and think of one of these happy thoughts. How does that sound?

JENNIFER: That sounds like something I can do. It would be nice to be able to snap myself out of some of those stressful times.

Commentary

Jennifer cooperated with the therapist and seemed to enjoy learning the push button technique. This technique is not only an effective strategy for decreasing her symptoms and meeting first order change goals, but also appeals to Jennifer's desire to exercise control over her environment and emotional state. Whereas Jennifer was agreeable to previous interventions probably reflecting the people-pleasing part of her maladaptive pattern, her cooperation here reflects the shift toward her more adaptive pattern. Jennifer is more flexible and open to new ideas, more motivated to implement interventions, and more confident that she can effect change in her pattern and symptoms.

Concluding Note

This chapter reviewed selections from sessions five, six, seven, and eight, which represent the middle of therapy and lead to the termination phase, covered in chapter 9. The push button technique is introduced to help the client replace unpleasant feeling states with more pleasant ones. The Social Interest Inventory-Short Form (SII-SF) is administered again to track changes in the client's level of social interest. Pattern shifting and symptom reduction continue and the client becomes ready to focus on relapse prevention and termination. Additionally, Jennifer began demonstrating third order change, ensuring that treatment gains will persist after therapy is complete.

References

Mosak, H. H. (1985). Interrupting a depression: The pushbutton technique. *Individual Psychology*, 41(2), 210–214.

Mosak, H. H., & Maniacci, M. (1998). *Tactics in counseling and psychotherapy.* Itasca, IL: F. E. Peacock.

9

Preparing for Termination and Beyond

Learning Objectives

In this chapter, you will learn the following:

1. Guidelines for successful treatment termination
2. How to review progress of both first and second order change goals
3. How to create a relapse prevention plan in collaboration with the client
4. How to collect post-treatment early recollections
5. A continuing case of how Adlerian pattern-focused therapy is practiced.

Recall that Jennifer received a referral for psychotherapy because she did not want medication for her depressive disorder as originally offered by her physician. In their first meeting, both client and therapist agreed to begin with therapy and, if necessary, to arrange for medication to be combined with therapy. Became of Jennifer's early responsiveness to therapy, combined treatment with medication was not needed. This progress continued in subsequent sessions.

This chapter presents the termination phase of Jennifer's therapy: sessions nine and ten. These final two sessions encompass critical components of effective Adlerian pattern-focused therapy. At this point in therapy, the focus shifts to termination and final assessment. The Social Interest Inventory-Short Form (SII-SF) is administered and post-therapy early recollections are collected. This chapter presents five guidelines for successful termination and describes two components, relapse prevention planning and review of progress, in detail. The chapter then presents highlights from sessions nine and ten, with commentary, to demonstrate techniques and review Jennifer's progress over the course of treatment. The first four sessions comprise the initial phase of therapy, while sessions five through eight represent the middle phase. Finally, the termination phase consists of sessions nine and ten. Table 9.1 summarizes the change that occurred between the intake session and session eight in the case of Jennifer.

TABLE 9.1 Summary of Change (Sessions 1–8)

Tasks	Indicators	Techniques
First order change	Decreased depression Increased motivation Decreased social withdrawal	Encouragement Acting "as if" (behavioral activation) Query sequence Adlerian ABC model Push button technique Self-monitoring
Second order change	Shift to a more adaptive pattern of being reasonably conscientious while maintaining effectiveness	Encouragement Query sequence Acting "as if" Reflecting "as if"
Social interest	Increased social interest as indicated by Jennifer's social behavior and 12-point increase on the SII-SF	Encouragement Acting "as if" (behavioral activation) Query sequence Role playing
Skills learned	Jennifer learns to control her mood states, employ alternative thoughts and behaviors, and monitor her moods and triggers	Encouragement Push button technique Query sequence Adlerian ABC model Self-monitoring

Termination

An essential requisite for therapists practicing Adlerian pattern-focused therapy is to successfully terminate therapy. Termination is a process in which an important relationship changes for the client. Clients react differently to termination depending largely on their patterns. Any obstacles to termination can be effectively anticipated and traversed with an accurate case conceptualization. An effective termination is characterized by five main tasks: (a) discussing termination and the client's related thoughts and feelings; (b) discussing progress and goal attainment; (c) creating a relapse prevention plan; (d) discussing continuing client growth; and (e) making provisions for future sessions or contact (Sperry, 2010).

Discussing Termination

The therapist first initiates a discussion about termination, eliciting the client's positive and negative responses. Client responses may vary and be complex. A client may feel proud of goals reached in therapy yet worried about the task of maintaining those gains after treatment has ended.

Review of Progress and Goals

The therapist helps the client review progress and achievement of treatment goals by listing treatment gains and comparing them to the list of mutually agreed-on goals created during the intake session. Both first and second order goals are reviewed, one at a time. The therapist can inquire about the extent to which the client deems he or she has met each goal, on a scale from 0–10. Goals that are partially reached still account for change and the client is encouraged to continue in the process of fully attaining those goals. The therapist then invites clients to explore new goals for personal growth after termination and which they might pursue on their own or with some therapeutic support (Sperry, 2010).

Relapse Prevention Plan

Relapse prevention helps clients anticipate and decrease the likelihood that symptoms or maladaptive behaviors will return after treatment. This task helps clients improve coping skills, relational skills, and self-efficacy (Marlatt & Gordon, 1985). Relapse prevention planning is a collaborative process that begins with identifying potential triggers to symptoms and behaviors (Marlatt & Gordon, 1985). Triggers may be interpersonal, intrapersonal, physical, or environmental and are thought to precede emotional and behavioral responses. Originating in the 12-step tradition, the acronym HALT (hungry, angry, lonely, tired) is a useful tool for identifying common triggers. Individuals often find that one or more of these is a stressor for them. Strategies for avoiding or coping with each trigger should be identified.

After identifying triggers, the therapist helps the client identify early warning signs that symptoms are returning, or maladaptive behaviors are on the horizon. Specific strategies for addressing each early warning sign should be identified. The client is also encouraged to keep up lifestyle changes that generally help maintain treatment gains and stave off relapse (Sperry, 2010).

Continuing Client Growth

Some clients may endeavor to surpass their initial goals and seek continued personal growth. The therapist should discuss these new goals and help the client plan a route for attaining them, such as a support group, referral to a specialized therapist, or other activities.

Provisions for Future Sessions

The therapist should discuss the possibility of follow-up sessions. Sessions can be scheduled at three or six-month intervals. In some cases, follow-up sessions might not be necessary. In this case, the therapist collaborates with the client to decide if follow-up is needed and can inform the client that he or she is always welcome to return or call if needed (Sperry, 2010).

TABLE 9.2 Session 9 Assessment Scores

Patient Health Questionnaire-9 (PHQ-9)	2 (minimal to no depression)
Outcome Rating Scale (ORS)	33 total: 9 individually, 7 interpersonally, 9 socially, 8 overall
Session Rating Scale (SRS)	40
Mood Scale	8
MI scores	Importance: 10
	Confidence: 9

Case of Jennifer—Session 9 Transcription

Jennifer's PHQ-9 score is lower at session nine and her ORS score continues to increase. In this session, the therapist helps Jennifer draft a relapse prevention plan in preparation for termination. Jennifer identifies triggers to both her depression symptoms and maladaptive pattern. Additionally, she identifies early warning signs that her depression is returning, or that her maladaptive pattern is being triggered, and lists specific strategies she can use to manage both triggers and early symptoms. Finally, the therapist evaluates Jennifer's motivation for implementing the relapse prevention plan. Select sections from this transcription are presented next.

THERAPIST: Can you tell me more about your rating for individual functioning?

JENNIFER: Pretty good, overall. I feel so much better than when I first started coming here. My mood has definitely changed and I'm really happy about that. I feel relieved.

THERAPIST: Good. So, your mood has been improving and you can notice a difference from when you first came in to see me?

JENNIFER: Yes, I really have. It's a great relief because I was worried I'd continue to feel depressed.

THERAPIST: Can you tell me more about your rating for the interpersonal category?

JENNIFER: Yes, getting out with friends was good. My parents have been pretty good about things on the phone recently. They haven't been nagging me as much. Overall, I'd say things are going well in that area.

Commentary

In this exchange, Jennifer discussed her parents again for the first time since session five. She reported that her overall mood is better and that her relationship with her parents has improved. Jennifer's increased social interest and belonging, over the course of therapy, now serves as a mitigating factor in her relationship with her parents.

THERAPIST: That's always good, to have something to look forward to. How about your overall rating?

JENNIFER: My overall rating is good. I've found that things aren't getting on my nerves as much. That's something I just took for granted before, that things and people will get on my nerves. I never realized how much control I actually have over it.

THERAPIST: Right. You're finding that you have a lot more control over your mood and irritability than you once thought. And, considerably more control over your pattern as well.

JENNIFER: That's true. I think a lot of people don't stop and think about what they can do to make things better or what they can take responsibility for. I always thought I was taking responsibility for my work and that should be enough, but now I see that it isn't. I have to think about my mood, too, or I can fall back into that unhealthy pattern.

Commentary

Jennifer raised some points that will be useful in creating a relapse prevention plan. She revealed her new understanding of her pattern and triggers. Jennifer's conscientious pattern makes her more likely to implement the alternative thoughts and behaviors reflective of her adaptive pattern as she desires to control her emotional state and environment. In this case, she can exercise adaptive and productive control over her reflexive responses. The result of this pattern change is expected to be apparent in Jennifer's post-treatment early recollections, which will be collected in session ten.

THERAPIST: That's very good. (pause) Now, Jennifer, we have reviewed your progress and I would agree you have progressed very well. You have been able to make some big changes in your symptoms and your unhealthy pattern, and this has been reflected in your daily functioning, your relationships, and your enjoyment of life. Now, I would like to work on a plan with you that can help you maintain the gains you've made. It's called relapse prevention.

JENNIFER: Okay, yes, I would like to keep this up, especially since I am feeling so much better.

THERAPIST: Okay, good. The first part of this relapse prevention plan is identifying things that trigger your symptoms. This could be a situation, like feeling lonely or having a lot of work to do. It could also be a particular place or even a person. Can you think of things that trigger your low mood? **(relapse prevention)**

JENNIFER: Yes, usually it's me being self-critical and focusing too much on something I did wrong or something that didn't turn out the way I wanted it to.

THERAPIST: Okay, so you find that when you are overly critical of yourself, that affects your mood. Is there anything else?

JENNIFER: Yes, I've learned that isolating myself really affects my mood. It's a bad cycle where I start feeling depressed and then I avoid people even more.

THERAPIST: Okay, so avoiding people and being isolated is another mood trigger for you. What factors might be related to you feeling decreased motivation?

JENNIFER: Um, I think mostly it's when I'm perfectionistic and over-conscientious and I get stuck on all the little details of a project. It makes the project seem impossible. Plus, it takes up all my time planning and trying to work out things that aren't that big a deal. Then, I spend a lot of time working but I don't really get much done and I feel really discouraged.

THERAPIST: Okay, so when your perfectionistic and over-conscientious pattern comes up and you find yourself overly focused on small details, you feel overwhelmed and you tire yourself out and use up your time working on things that don't advance your project too much. That leads to you feeling discouraged and less motivated.

JENNIFER: Yes. That's what happens.

THERAPIST: So, as we discuss that pattern of perfectionism that brings excess focus on details, criticism, and irritability being a trigger for your mood symptoms, what are some things that trigger that pattern?

JENNIFER: Hmm. I think one big trigger is when I know I'm going to be evaluated on something important. Like if a paper or project is a big part of my grade in a class. Also, when I have to work and coordinate with other people. Working with people on a group project can be hard. Also trying to coordinate outings with people. I tend to get annoyed and irritated in those situations. It's good that I learned that about myself here, so I can deal with it more effectively.

THERAPIST: Good. So, I'm hearing triggers for your pattern are being evaluated on an important project and coordinating work and social events with others. Is that right?

JENNIFER: Yes, that's right.

THERAPIST: Okay, now that we have identified your triggers, let's talk about some of your early warning signs. How do you know when you are starting to feel depressed?

JENNIFER: Um, mostly I feel apathetic or irritable. I feel like I don't want to do anything. Everything gets on my nerves. I just want to be left alone, and I find things are not so enjoyable anymore.

THERAPIST: You find yourself starting to feel apathetic as well as feeling irritated by most things.

JENNIFER: That's right.

THERAPIST: Now, what are some of the early signs that let you know your pattern of perfectionism is coming back into play?

JENNIFER: Hmm. That's harder to figure out. I guess mostly I start to feel frustrated, annoyed, irritated. Usually it only takes something small to irritate me.

THERAPIST: So, when you notice your threshold for being irritated, frustrated, or annoyed is lower, a sign of your pattern is coming up?

JENNIFER: Yes, I would say so.

THERAPIST: A helpful acronym people often use to understand their triggers is called HALT. That stands for hungry, angry, lonely, and tired. Those are very common triggers for many people. Do any of those stand out as possible triggers to your maladaptive pattern? **(HALT)**

JENNIFER: Yes, actually. That is interesting. I would say definitely angry, lonely, or tired. When I'm lonely, that triggers my depression. When I'm angry or tired, I think my old pattern is triggered more.

THERAPIST: Okay, good. I am glad that you were able to identify those. Now that we have identified your triggers and some early warning signs for your mood and pattern, what are some strategies you can use when you recognize these early signs, to prevent things from getting worse?

JENNIFER: Um, well, like we discussed, the push button technique.

THERAPIST: So, using the push button technique when you find yourself feeling irritated or apathetic, as you described?

JENNIFER: Yes. And the alternative thoughts and behaviors, especially the thoughts. Thinking of those can really help me.

THERAPIST: Stopping and examining your thoughts and behaviors and generating some more helpful alternatives. As you said earlier, you found you are able to turn some of your days around and change your mood this way.

JENNIFER: Yes, it really works, so that is something I can do. I also like using affirmations. Those have been helpful and easy to use.

THERAPIST: Great. Affirmations can be something you continue to use. Is there anything else?

JENNIFER: Exercising seems to help. It really helps my mood when I'm upset. So does actually going out with my friends. I find that I'm a lot better overall when I find time to relax and spend time with people.

THERAPIST: That sounds like a good plan. It is helpful to have a specific plan as well. When you feel your low mood is being triggered, is there something specific you can do at that moment?

JENNIFER: Um, I guess I can call a friend.

THERAPIST: That's a great idea. Who would be a good person to call when you're in a jam?

JENNIFER: Probably my friend Stephanie. Or Debra. They're both usually there when I need someone.

THERAPIST: Okay, so you will call Stephanie or Debra when you feel some of those early warning signs of your depression?

JENNIFER: Yes.

THERAPIST: How about when you feel your maladaptive pattern starting to come back?

JENNIFER: I guess I can go exercise to clear my head and then use some of those alternatives.

THERAPIST: That sounds like a great plan. You have mentioned before that both exercising and socializing have been things that improved your mood as well as your perfectionistic pattern.

JENNIFER: Yes, I think I can keep these things up.

THERAPIST: On a scale from 0 to 10, how important is it for you to implement this relapse prevention plan and maintain the progress you have made?

JENNIFER: I would definitely say 10. I can see how much this has helped me and I want to keep it up.

THERAPIST: Okay, that is good news. On the same scale, how confident are you that you can implement this plan?

JENNIFER: I would say 8. I am confident I can do it, but I know how busy the semester can get and so that's something I will have to work with.

THERAPIST: Okay, good. What do you think it might take to bump that to a 9 or a 10?

JENNIFER: I think if I can keep it up the next couple of weeks, which are really busy, then I'll feel a lot more confident that I will make it a key part of my recovery. Particularly since I see how it will help me act out of my adaptive pattern rather than out of my unhealthy pattern.

THERAPIST: Wonderful insight.

JENNIFER: I'm beginning to feel really hopeful.

THERAPIST: Great. I'm really happy for you (Pause). Okay, so if you can show yourself that you can keep up the things you have learned in our sessions, after we conclude therapy, and even when you are busy, that will help you to feel more confident about your ability to maintain your progress long term?

JENNIFER: Yes, I think so.

Commentary

Jennifer was an active participant in creating the relapse prevention plan and was agreeable to the process. She identified specific triggers for her mood, decreased motivation, and pattern, as well as early warning signs that her depressive symptoms and maladaptive pattern are resurfacing. Additionally, she identified specific strategies to use to cope with triggers and warning signs. The therapist was careful to have Jennifer identify several specific, rather than vague or general, strategies to use in certain situations. Having a defined plan means Jennifer will be more likely to employ these strategies and maintain her treatment gains. Table 9.3 outlines Jennifer's relapse prevention plan.

TABLE 9.3 Jennifer's Relapse Prevention Plan

Plan/ Three goals:	**Triggers**	**Warning signs**	**Strategies**
1. Mood	Self-criticism	Apathy	Push button technique
	Ruminating on errors/shortcomings	Irritability	Alternative thoughts and behaviors
			Exercise
	Isolation/social withdrawal		Socializing
	HALT: lonely		Calling a friend
2. Motivation	Perfectionism	Apathy	Encouragement
	Excessive focus on details	Irritability	Alternative thoughts and behaviors
3. Pattern	Being evaluated	Frustration	Alternative thoughts and behaviors
	Working with others	Annoyance	
	HALT (angry and tired)	Irritability	

Case of Jennifer—Session 10 Transcription

Session ten marks the completion of therapy. Jennifer's improvement is evident in her PHQ-9, ORS, and Mood Scale scores. Additionally, her SII-SF score at session ten is 28 points higher than it was at the intake session, a marked increase. This session is dedicated to reviewing goals and the relapse prevention plan and collecting post-therapy early recollections. Each goal is reviewed individually and rated for level of achievement on a 0–10 scale. The therapist helps Jennifer reflect on what she learned over the course of therapy and what new goals she would like to set for future personal growth. Post-therapy early recollections are collected in a similar way as pre-treatment recollections. Select sections from this transcription are presented next. Chapter 10 provides an analysis of these post-treatment early recollections.

TABLE 9.4 Session 10 Assessment Scores

Patient Health Questionnaire-9 (PHQ-9)	1 (minimal to no depression)
Outcome Rating Scale (ORS)	34 total: 9 individually, 8 interpersonally, 8 socially, 9 overall
Session Rating Scale (SRS)	40
Mood Scale	9
Social Interest Inventory-Short Form (SII-SF)	49

THERAPIST: Okay, that's very good. That brings us to our next point. I would like to discuss the goals we set when you first came in and see the extent to which you have met them. How does that sound? **(review progress on treatment goals)**

JENNIFER: Yes, okay. That sounds good.

THERAPIST: Ok, good. One of your goals was to improve your mood. On a scale from 0 to 10, how much do you feel you have attained that goal?

JENNIFER: I would say 9. My mood has been a lot better. I feel so relieved. I was really feeling bad for some time and I can definitely tell the difference.

THERAPIST: Can you tell me more about that?

JENNIFER: Yes, I would wake up feeling really depressed and have this general feeling like the day was going to be pretty blue. I just felt like I was in a rut and dragging along. I felt really irritated a lot. I don't feel that way now. I feel so much better. Not even like my old self, actually better.

THERAPIST: That is good to hear. I am very glad to hear that you have experienced this change in your mood and you are feeling the way you want to feel. Your next goal was to increase your motivation. How much would you say you have met that goal?

JENNIFER: Probably a 9 also. I have been feeling a lot more motivated lately. It seems like the more I do, the more I feel like doing. It's like I can get in the swing of things and then it takes a life of its own. I feel like I can handle more, too, and I am actually enjoying myself when I go out. I was really dragging before.

THERAPIST: I am glad to hear you are feeling more motivated and enjoying yourself more. Your third goal was to enjoy more activities. How much would you say you have met that goal?

JENNIFER: I would say 8. I can't always enjoy myself because I'm busy a lot so there's not a lot of time for fun. But, I felt so low before that I felt apathetic. Like things didn't matter that much. And I didn't have fun, even when I did go out and do things. I've definitely enjoyed myself a lot more these last few weeks and I'm so glad for that. I really need those times when I get to have fun and relax. Before I came in to see you, it felt like everything was a chore so I never actually got any stress relief.

THERAPIST: Because you were getting little to no pleasure from the activities you were doing?

JENNIFER: Yes, that's right. So, I feel relieved that I was able to meet this goal. It was really important to me.

THERAPIST: I am happy to hear this and that you are enjoying yourself again and getting some much-needed enjoyment and relief from your stress. (pause) What about the goal of changing your pattern of being perfectionistic and becoming too focused on details to the point where it interferes with what you want to do? On a scale from 0 to 10, how much have you met that goal?

JENNIFER: I would say an 8. I am definitely finding that I can let stuff go more often. Or that I can stay focused on the big picture. It's easier to get my work done because I'm not sidetracked so much by small details and I'm not so easily frustrated by things or even other people any more.

THERAPIST: I am glad to hear this. It seems you have been able to make some big changes to help yourself feel better and create more of what you want in your life.

Commentary

Jennifer gave high ratings for attainment of her goals. Her ratings are representative of her shift to a more adaptive pattern of being reasonably conscientious. Had Jennifer not shifted to an adaptive pattern, her self-criticism and rigid standards would have led to her rating her progress more harshly. Jennifer's ratings are likely less than 10 because of her attention to detail and current stress from school, which is to be expected. Table 9.5 outlines Jennifer's goal achievement.

JENNIFER: Thank you. I definitely feel that way. I really didn't think about a lot of these things before I came here and started talking to you, but now I see how they were holding me back. I would say I'm less perfectionistic now. I still have certain standards for things and I really want to do my work well, but I've just realized that nothing can ever actually be perfect, so really, I'm just getting myself upset for nothing. That was probably one of the major takeaways, that I really have a choice as to whether I am going to get upset or feel bad. Especially with the push button and reflecting "as if" techniques you taught me. It feels good to know that I have control over my moods, and just because something happens or I wake up in a bad mood, that doesn't have to ruin my day or my week.

THERAPIST: Ok, so practicing the push button and reflecting "as if" techniques has shown you how you can control your moods and that is something you feel you have been able to use to your advantage.

JENNIFER: Yes, for sure. For example, before I would wake up in a bad mood and think, "Okay, this is going to be a bad day. I can't believe it's another bad day." And I would just be irritated and annoyed all day. Now I think, "I can turn this day around." And I find that I actually can change my mood. Sometimes it's a little more difficult, but I don't have to have an entire day lost to a bad mood. I can turn it around **(third order change)**.

THERAPIST: So, you have found a way to change your thinking and change your moods instead of allowing your moods to dictate your days.

JENNIFER: Yes, that's a good way to put it.

THERAPIST: What was the most important change for you in regards to your daily functioning?

JENNIFER: Um, I would say being able to stop and think of alternative thoughts and behaviors when I'm feeling upset or overwhelmed. That has been so helpful.

THERAPIST: Can you give me an example?

JENNIFER: Um, yes. The other day, my friend texted me to see if I wanted to hang out. It was Saturday, but I had homework to do. I got really annoyed with her. I told her I couldn't go but then I was still upset that she had even asked and I had a hard time concentrating on my work. And so I stopped and tried to figure out what I was thinking and I realized I was thinking,

"She's such a slacker. Doesn't she realize that some people actually have work to do?" Then I was able to get some perspective and realize it was a weekend and we don't all have the same classes. It was actually nice of her to think of me and see if I wanted to hang out. I felt a lot better after that and was able to focus on my work again (third order change).

THERAPIST: Okay, so you were able to stop and think about what thoughts were going through your head that may have been contributing to your feelings. And then you were able to redirect yourself and come up with some alternative thoughts, and you found you were able to affect your mood and concentration that way.

JENNIFER: Yes, that's right.

Commentary

Jennifer described a situation that triggered her mood and one that triggered her maladaptive pattern. She was able, however, to implement her relapse prevention plan to identify triggers and early warning signs. She then used the push button technique to ameliorate her mood and employed alternative thoughts and behaviors to stave off her maladaptive pattern. These two instances constitute third order change and serve to increase Jennifer's self-efficacy and the likelihood that she will maintain treatment gains and avoid relapse.

THERAPIST: I am glad to hear that you were able to use these techniques to your advantage and that you've seen some measurable changes in your life as a result. What would you say you have learned about yourself through this process?

JENNIFER: I guess I didn't really realize how perfectionistic I was before and how much it was getting in my way. I never thought I was perfectionistic because I never felt like I met my own standards. So, because I never achieved perfection, I felt like that meant I wasn't perfectionistic or too obsessed with details and stuff.

THERAPIST: Okay, so you learned a lot about yourself and your patterns. You were able to see that you have some perfectionistic tendencies and that they actually hinder your performance instead of enhancing it.

JENNIFER: Yes, for sure. I also learned that I can be kind of critical of people sometimes. Sometimes I lose my patience. And then every time I've looked at that more closely, I see that I can actually understand where the other person is coming from. It's all about slowing down and not getting caught up in my thoughts, like we talked about earlier.

THERAPIST: Okay, so you've found that sometimes you can be unnecessarily critical of others and you have also found that you have the ability to control that by choosing alternative thoughts.

JENNIFER: Yes.

THERAPIST: Do you notice any change in your feelings toward relationships with those people as a result?

JENNIFER: Yes, I definitely do. I feel a lot more understanding and sympathetic. My relationships have improved because I'm not as irritated with people. I found I am able to go out more and hang out with friends more if I can change my thinking about some of their behaviors. Basically, not holding my friends to some of those perfectionistic standards either.

THERAPIST: That's good. I'm glad that you were able to enrich some of your relationships in addition to alleviating your mood. What else would you like to change about yourself from here on out?

JENNIFER: Um, I would like to be able to be more spontaneous. Not all the time, not to the point of being impulsive like some people are. But there are times I think being spontaneous would be really fun and feel good. I usually like to have things planned so that can be hard for me.

THERAPIST: Can you give me an example of what being more spontaneous would look like?

JENNIFER: Yes, a couple of weeks ago, there was an opportunity to take a weekend trip to a museum with one of my classes. Everyone was going to stay in a hotel Friday and Saturday night and have time to explore the city. I was on the waiting list for the trip and the spot opened up last minute. I declined because I felt like I didn't have enough time and it was overwhelming. Now, I wish I had gone. It would be nice to sometimes just do something like that even though it's not planned.

THERAPIST: That sounds like a good goal. Do you think you will be able to use some of the techniques you've learned here to help you achieve that goal?

JENNIFER: Yes, I think so. I have gotten a lot better at finding those alternative thoughts and behaviors, so I think I can transfer those skills to this area.

Commentary

Jennifer identified what she learned about herself through the therapy process. Her ability to objectively discuss her perfectionism and maladaptive pattern points to her shift to a more adaptive pattern. In this interaction, Jennifer was able to examine herself and her behaviors without triggering her self-criticism. She also reported a new goal would be to be more spontaneous.

This goal represents a major shift from her maladaptive pattern as it far surpasses her initial goal of just being more reasonably conscientious. Finally, this goal of spontaneity indicates her increased social interest and her continuing desire to connect with others, as it has been a rewarding experience thus far.

THERAPIST:	Let's shift gears a bit now. (pause). Please tell me one of your earliest recollections. It should be something before age eight, that you remember happening, rather than something someone told you. **(early recollection 1)**
JENNIFER:	Yes, when I was six, I spent all week making a tower out of these toy bricks my parents bought me. I worked so hard on it and spent a long time planning it. It got really tall. But then when I came home from school one day, I found my sister had knocked it down. I got so mad at my sister and my mom had to come break it up. But she felt bad for me and she helped me put it back together.
THERAPIST:	Okay, so you made a tower out of toy bricks and your sister knocked it down and then your mother helped you rebuild it. Is that right?
JENNIFER:	Yes, we actually spent a long time doing it together.
THERAPIST:	What is the most vivid part of that memory?
JENNIFER:	Probably working with my mom to rebuild it. It was a fun time and really relaxing. I remember laughing a lot with her and she gave me a hug and told me I did a good job.
THERAPIST:	What do you remember thinking?
JENNIFER:	I thought it was really nice that my mom was helping me and supporting me. She paid attention to how upset I felt and that was nice.
THERAPIST:	And how did you feel?
JENNIFER:	I felt good. Happy, loved, and appreciated.
THERAPIST:	Please tell me another recollection **(early recollection 2)**
JENNIFER:	Um, I remember when I was eight I had a speech to give in my forensics class. I practiced it for an hour every day. Then one day my forensics teacher told me that I was chosen to present at the all-school variety show. It went well.
THERAPIST:	Okay, so you worked really hard on this speech for school and practiced for an hour every day and then were told you were selected to present at the variety show. Is that right?

JENNIFER: Yes, that's right.

THERAPIST: What is the most vivid part of that memory?

JENNIFER: Um, being told I was chosen to present. That was really cool.

THERAPIST: Okay. And what do you remember thinking?

JENNIFER: I was really proud that I was able to accomplish that and I didn't lose balance in my life. I didn't get obsessed over it. I was able to practice a lot but not go crazy. I was able to still do other things I needed and wanted to do.

THERAPIST: Okay, and how did you feel?

JENNIFER: I felt excited and really grateful that I was chosen. That was a really great experience for me. It meant a lot to me.

Commentary

See chapter 10 for an analysis of Jennifer's post-treatment early recollections and comparison to the pre-treatment ones.

THERAPIST: That's very good. Let's review your relapse prevention plan from last session. **(relapse prevention plan)**

JENNIFER: Sure. I'm really glad we came up with that plan.

THERAPIST: So, let's review your triggers first. I wrote down that your key triggers are situations where you are likely to respond with perfectionism, self-criticalness, or isolating yourself.

JENNIFER: Yes, that's right. I think I have to be more aware of when I start doing that stuff. Now that I realize how it's connected to my mood, I've realized it's important not to let those things go.

THERAPIST: Can you tell me more about that?

JENNIFER: Yes. I used to not do much about it when I was isolating or being perfectionistic. Because I didn't see it as connected to my mood before, I didn't feel like it was that important to deal with those things. Now, I realize that I have to pay more attention and make some changes when I notice those triggers because it affects my mood so much.

THERAPIST: That's a very good insight. That brings us to some of your early warning signs. You said you start to feel apathetic and irritable when you are starting to feel depressed.

JENNIFER: Yes, that's true. Now I know that when I start to feel that way, I need to use some of the strategies I learned here so it doesn't get worse.

THERAPIST: And which strategies will you use?

JENNIFER: I think the push button technique and some of the affirmations would be a good start.

THERAPIST: I think so, too. You also mentioned in our last session that you notice your threshold for feeling irritated or annoyed gets lower when your pattern is triggered.

JENNIFER: Yes. I think it's good to know that about myself because now I realize I can do something about it. It doesn't have to be something that just happens and that I can't control.

THERAPIST: So, realizing you have control over your mood and your pattern has been helpful to you.

JENNIFER: Definitely. I like having something I can do about the situation.

THERAPIST: Okay, good. Going over your relapse prevention plan, I am glad to hear you feel hopeful about your progress and your ability to maintain it. In the informed consent you signed when you first came here, there was a provision for further follow-up sessions if necessary. Based on our review of your progress today, it seems like you have made the most of our work together and are really doing well, so follow-up sessions in the near future do not seem necessary. Would you agree?

JENNIFER: Yes, I would agree with that. I got more out of these sessions than I ever thought I would. I didn't know there were so many tools a person could use to deal with depression and stress. It had not occurred to me before that I could change the way I approach work, or people, or just life in general. All this without medication!

THERAPIST: Yes, all these changes without medication! It sounds like you feel a lot more empowered now that you have experienced how much control you have over your moods, your thoughts, and your behaviors. However, if down the road, things seems to be really getting you down and the strategies don't seem to be working, please know you can get in touch with me at the clinic, here.

JENNIFER: (Pause). Yes, I like having that option. Thank you.

THERAPIST: Okay, Jennifer. I am really glad that you have made so much progress and that you feel empowered seeing yourself make these changes that have been so important for you. I have really enjoyed our time together and seeing you grow.

JENNIFER: Thank you. I have really enjoyed working with you. I really learned a lot and I felt comfortable enough to share what I was going through.

THERAPIST: Thank you!

Commentary

To conclude, the therapist reviewed Jennifer's relapse prevention plan once again and gaged Jennifer's readiness for termination. The possibility of future sessions was discussed and a course of action was agreed on. Jennifer terminated therapy having achieved both first and second order goals and was highly motivated to maintain her gains and prevent future relapse. See Table 9.5 for a summary of Jennifer's goal ratings.

TABLE 9.5 Jennifer's Goal Rating

Goal	Rating (0–10)
Improve mood	9
Increase motivation	9
Increase pleasure/enjoyment	8
Move to adaptive pattern	8

Concluding Note

At the outset of this chapter, it was noted that Jennifer received a referral for psychotherapy because she did not want medication. Because of her early responsiveness to therapy and positive changes in her mood, medication was not needed. This chapter reviews the final two sessions of Jennifer's planned 10-session therapy.

This chapter describes the termination phase of therapy. It began with a review of progress and included the creation of a relapse prevention plan. Considerable progress toward both first and second order goals was noted, and the therapist helped the client identify triggers and early warning signs for both primary symptoms and the maladaptive pattern. A strategy for coping with triggers and symptoms after termination was then mutually agreed on by client and therapist. This was followed by discussion of other goals for continued personal growth and the possibility of future sessions while mutually agreeing on a termination plan for the client.

References

Marlatt, G. A., Gordon, J. R., (1985) *Relapse prevention: Maintenance strategies in the treatment of addictive behaviors.* New York, NY: Guilford Press

Sperry, L. (2010). *Highly effective therapy: Developing essential clinical competencies in counseling and psychotherapy.* New York, NY: Routledge.

10

Markers of a Successful Therapy and the Future of Adlerian Therapy

Learning Objectives

In this chapter, you will learn the following:

1. The six markers of successful therapy
2. The six markers in Jennifer's successful therapy
3. Early recollections are another marker of Jennifer's successful therapy
4. The accomplishments and challenges facing of Adlerian therapy

Jennifer did complete a 10-session course of Adlerian pattern-focused therapy. By all measures, including her own personal evaluation, the therapy was successful. Recall that she was referred by her physician for therapy because she did not want medication for her depressive symptoms. Fortunately, like others who are responsive to focused therapy that directly addresses depressive symptoms, she was able to successfully complete therapy without adding medication to the treatment plan.

So what accounts for successful therapy in general, and then, specifically, what accounted for success in the case of Jennifer? This chapter addresses both questions. It begins with a discussion of the markers or criteria of successful therapy. Then, it shows how Jennifer's therapy met each of these criteria. Next, it reviews the changes in early recollections collected in the first and last sessions. Specifically, it interprets these changes and reflects on how they "confirm" the shift from Jennifer's maladaptive pattern to a more adaptive pattern. Finally, the future of Adlerian therapy is discussed in terms of accomplishment and challenges.

Indicators of Successful Therapy

While there is yet no definitive research on exactly how therapy effects deep and lasting change in clients, six markers and criteria of successful or highly effective therapy have been described (Goldfried, 2012; Sperry & Carlson, 2014). They are enhancing the therapeutic alliance, fostering positive expectations and client motivation, identifying patterns and treatment focus, increasing client awareness, fostering corrective experiences, and facilitating first, second, and third order change. This section describes all six indicators. Also noted is how these markers were operative in the case of Jennifer

Enhancing the Therapeutic Alliance

The therapeutic alliance is the bond between client and therapist as well as agreement on the goals of therapy and the methods of achieving them (Bordin, 1994). A productive therapeutic alliance enhances clients' trust that their therapist is competent and is interested in their well-being (Sperry & Carlson, 2014). Therapeutic alliances vary from client to client. Accordingly, a therapist may rather easily develop a bond with a motivated client or may exert considerable effort and clinical skills in developing and maintaining an effective alliance with an unmotivated or defiant client. Enhancing the therapeutic alliance fosters the client's involvement in therapy and his or her willingness to engage in the often painful process of change (Goldfried, 2012).

In Jennifer's therapy, the therapeutic alliance appeared to develop with relative ease and with limited resistance. In large part, this was due to her level of motivation, and because of the therapist's expertise in fostering a productive alliance, particularly with ongoing encouragement and by anticipating possible transference and authority issues. In reviewing her family history, particularly the critical and demanding behavior of her mother, the therapist anticipated that this dynamic might arise in the alliance with Jennifer. Accordingly, the therapist, a female somewhat older than Jennifer, was intentional in her efforts to not activate that transference but instead to respond to Jennifer in a caring and non-demanding manner.

Fostering Client Motivation and Positive Expectations

For therapeutic change to occur, clients need a reasonable level of motivation for change, as well as the expectation that therapy will help them. When motivation and expectations are low, the therapist's immediate task is to enhance or increase both of these essential prerequisites (Goldfried, 2012). Therapists may use motivational interviewing or other interventions to increase motivation and readiness for change, as well as enhance the expectation that therapy will be effective.

Jennifer's therapy showed a relatively high degree of motivation and realistic expectations, which the therapist continually supported and enhanced. Because Jennifer was clear that she wanted talk therapy rather than medication, and because her depressive symptoms were in the low moderate range, her expectations were a good match for this therapy. The use of the two key motivational interviewing questions (i.e., importance of changing her maladaptive pattern and her level of confidence in achieving it) were utilized in each session to increase motivation and readiness for change.

Identifying Patterns and Focus Treatment

"Most patients readily accept the idea that there is a 'pattern' underlying their behavior. The word is reassuring, for it suggests that there is order and meaning to behavior and experience. Educating patients about these patterns helps them to distance themselves from events and promotes self-observation. At the same time, pattern recognition promotes integration by connecting, events, behaviors, and experiences that were previously assumed to be unconnected" (Livesley, p. 274). A key value of developing and sharing a clear an accurate case conceptualization is that it helps clients identify ineffective patterns and shift to more adaptive patterns (Sperry & Sperry, 2012).

Treatment focus provides directionality to treatment and aims at replacing a maladaptive pattern with a more adaptive pattern (Sperry, 2010). One of the best ways of keeping treatment focused is to track or monitor it with ultra-brief assessment measures. In this case, measures such as PHQ-9 and SII-SF were utilized. Not surprisingly, focusing and tracking treatment are not optional, but are essential in effective time-limited therapy.

Jennifer's treatment was intentionally focused on her pattern. From the second session through the tenth session, the pattern-focused case conceptualization was developed by the therapist and shared and accepted by Jennifer. This case conceptualization guided and infused the treatment process. She fully agreed that her maladaptive pattern "drove" her depression and readily participated in therapeutic process to shift the pattern to a more adaptive one. Besides keeping therapy focused on Jennifer's life strategy or pattern, the therapist maintained and monitored the productive treatment focus with the ongoing use of the following measures: mood scale, PHQ-9, SRS, and ORS at each session; and the SII-SF at the first, fifth, and last sessions.

Increasing Client Awareness

Increasing clients' awareness is another indicator of change. Irrespective of the therapist's orientation, awareness is needed for change to be effective. "Some clients may be unaware of how their thinking is influencing their feelings, others may be unaware of how their emotional reaction results in behavior, and still others how their behavior negatively impacts on others. Thus, individuals who are unaware of their anger, and their tendency to withdraw when angry may be unaware of how this emotion-action links adversely affects their relationships with others" (Goldfried, 2012, p. 20).

Increasing client awareness involves several therapeutic considerations such as the frequency type of thoughts, feelings, and behaviors. Sharing a clear and accurate case conceptualization with the client can greatly foster such awareness. By understanding their maladaptive pattern, clients are better able to make sense of the factors influencing their life.

The focus of Jennifer's therapy greatly facilitated her awareness. First, she became aware of the daily life situations and thoughts that triggered her maladaptive pattern of perfectionism and over-conscientiousness. Next, she became increasingly aware of how pattern both triggered her depressive symptoms and then exacerbated them. Subsequently, such awareness was critical in her decision to shift away from that pattern.

Facilitating Corrective Experiences

Beyond awareness, insight, or simple behavior change, effective change can and often requires a corrective experience. Corrective experiences are those in which individuals can re-experience an event or relationship in a different and unexpected manner. Such corrective experiences can disconfirm past negative experiences and effect profound changes (Castonguay & Hill, 2012). Such experiences represent second order change and play a central role in the transformative processes of various psychotherapy approaches. One clear indicator that a corrective emotional, cognitive, or relational experience has occurred is "when clients report a between-session experience with the tone of surprise in their voice—either because they behaved in a way that was different for them or because of the unexpected positive consequences that followed what they did. At other times, the (corrective experience) may result from ongoing interaction with a supportive and affirming therapist" (Goldfried, 2012, p. 21).

Jennifer's therapy provided emotional, cognitive, and relational corrective experiences. The corrective emotional one was evident in her increased self-acceptance, while the corrective cognitive experience was reflected in her shift to the more adaptive pattern. Corrective experience also extended to her relationships. This included an encouraging and affirming—rather than demanding—relationship with her therapist. It also appears to have translated to more positive relationships with other authority figures in her life, including her professors at her university and quite possibly her parents.

Facilitating First, Second, and Third Order Change

Therapy change has been identified in terms of three orders or levels of change (Good & Beitman, 2006). First order change involves small changes such as reducing symptoms or achieving stability. While appropriate for crisis counseling, medications management, and case management, this level is not sufficient for psychotherapy. Second order change is transformative (Fraser & Solovey, 2007) and occurs with a shift from a maladaptive pattern to a more adaptive one. A therapist always mediates this level of change. In contrast, third order change results from the client's own efforts without the assistance of a therapist. Basically, clients become their own therapists. Long term, enduring change requires some degree of third order change (Sperry & Carlson, 2014). If the goal of treatment is deep and lasting change, the focus of therapy must be on second and third order change, as first order change is insufficient.

Jennifer's therapy included the accomplishment of both first order goals and second order goals, and some indication of third order change goals. The first order goals accomplished involved her mood and daily functioning. As her depressive symptoms ameliorated, her mood improved and she had more energy and increased motivation. She was able to enjoy life and friends more than in the past. The second order goal achieved was her shift to the more adaptive pattern of being more reasonably conscientious and less perfectionistic. There was also some third order change. Jennifer used the query strategy on herself in some situations between sessions. In the final session, she identifies other ways in which her old pattern affected her and set a goal to be more spontaneous following therapy.

Not all clients will respond to therapy to the extent that Jennifer did. Major therapeutic change requires much of both client and therapist. On the client's part, readiness and willingness to change the capacity to relate to the therapist and the presence of strengths and protective factors (Sperry & Carlson, 2014) are essential. On the therapist's part, sufficient expertise in achieving the six criteria of highly effective therapy is equally essential. From my (LS) experience supervising therapists over the past four decades, three of these are absolutely essential in fostering change in difficult-to-treat clients. They are developing a facilitative therapeutic alliance, formulating accurate and complete case conceptualizations, and effectively tailoring and implementing interventions.

Early Recollections: First and Last Session

As noted earlier, early recollections are a projective technique in which early memories are used to identify an individual's lifestyle convictions or self-other schema, life strategy, and personal pattern, whether maladaptive or adaptive. Adlerian therapists view recollections as stories shaped by the individual's *current* view of self, others, and the world. Over the course of therapy, recollections can and do change (Clark, 2002; Mosak & DiPietro, 2006). Early recollections collected at the outset of therapy are called pre-intervention ERs, while those collected near the end of therapy are referred to as post-intervention ERs. "Changes in ERs frequently occur in therapy and these changes appear to be in accord with our clients' changed perception of life" (Mosak & DiPietro, 2006, p. 203). In our experience, pre- to post-intervention changes also include changes in life strategy (i.e., from a maladaptive pattern to a more adaptive pattern). As therapy focuses on shifting the maladaptive pattern to a more adaptive one, the client's self-other schemas (i.e., self-view and world-view) also shift in a healthier direction, even though the therapeutic focus is on the life strategy and not self-other schemas. In this section, we review the two sets of early recollections and interpret them, and then note how they reflect Jennifer's maladaptive and more adaptive patterns.

Let's begin by reviewing her pre-therapy recollections. As you may recall, she reported two ERs in the first session. The first was at age six. She said: "I spent several hours a day over the course of a week building a tall tower with toy bricks. I came home from school the next day to find that my little sister had knocked it down. I pushed her down and my parents punished me by taking a privilege away from me." What was most vivid for her was "seeing my tower all over the floor." In response, she reported feeling "upset and angry but didn't show it" and thinking "It's ruined. My sister makes trouble for me and I get punished. It's not fair."

The second was at age eight. She said: "I was playing my violin solo at our school's music recital and I made two small mistakes. Afterwards, my parents yelled at me for not practicing enough." What was most vivid was "making the mistakes." What was most vivid for her was "In response, she reported feeling "embarrassed, sad, and worried" and thinking "I worked so hard and I failed. I can't stand it."

We interpreted these pre-therapy recollections as consistent with her obsessive-compulsive pattern of achievement, perfectionism, and over-conscientiousness. In the first one, her hard work is "ruined" and she is punished for "moving against" her sister. The second one seemed to foreshadow her depressive response to overly high demands and lack of emotional support from others. We noted that both these recollections were consistent with and confirmed Jennifer's maladaptive pattern of overconscientiousness and perfectionistic striving that interferes with completing tasks.

Let's now review her post-therapy recollections. Two were reported in the tenth session. The first was at age six. She said: "I made a high tower with Legos. The next day I came home from school and found that it had been knocked down by my little sister. But, my mom helped me put it back together." What was most vivid for her was "working with my mom to rebuild it." In response, she reported feeling "good" and thinking "it's nice to get mom's help and emotional support."

The second was at age eight. She said: "I practiced my forensics speech for an hour every day. Then I was told by the forensics teacher that I was chosen to present it at the all-school variety show." What was most vivid for her was "being told I was chosen to present." In response, she reported feeling "excited and grateful" and thinking "I was able to accomplish this without losing getting obsessive and losing balance in my life."

Jennifer's second set of early recollections rather clearly reflect changes made over the course of therapy. Not only does she no longer experience depressive symptoms, but her early recollections reveal more balanced and healthy self-other schemas (self-view and world view).

These changes in early recollections are also consistent with the observed shift or change to a more adaptive life strategy or pattern. Whereas the pre-therapy observed pattern and recollections reflect an overly conscientious and perfectionistic striving, her more adaptive pattern was one of being reasonably conscientious and task focused, as well as less perfectionistic. She always exhibited more balance and greater satisfaction with life.

Two questions often are asked about therapeutic changes in early recollections. The first is "How is it that individuals appear to be injecting new and more positive meaning in a second recollection of the same event?" The answer is that, by definition, recollections are not exact memories of a past situation but rather reflections of the individual's perceptions of his or her life in the present. Of importance is that they may be more positive and healthy if the individual has, in fact, become more healthy and positive. A second question is "How is it that individuals give a much different second post-therapy recollection that has nothing to do with the first? In this case, the reason is that Jennifer is less focused on her obsessive pattern of over-conscientiousness, perfectionism, and negative evaluation. Instead, because she is now more focused on being reasonably conscientious and less concerned about positive evaluation by herself and others, the music memory is no longer at the forefront of her thinking. Instead, she reports on the positive recollection of being notified of participation in the school's variety show.

PHQ-9 and SII-SF

Finally, let's compare two of the measures that were collected over the course of therapy with the interpretations of Jennifer's early recollections. You'll recall that a measure of major depressive disorder, PHQ-9, was collected before each session. This, of course, is a marker of progress toward the first order treatment goal. The lower the score, the fewer symptoms and criteria of major depressive disorders. You may also recall that Social Interest Index-Short Form (SII-SF) was collected at the first, fifth, and tenth sessions. The higher the score, the higher the level of social interest. The expectation is that if therapy is effective, not only should early recollections become more healthy and adaptive, the level of social interest should increase.

In fact, this is what happened in Jennifer's therapy. See Figure 10.1, which visually illustrates this change, with PHQ-9 sloping downward and SII-SF sloping upward.

FIGURE 10.1. Change in depressive symptoms and social interest scores.

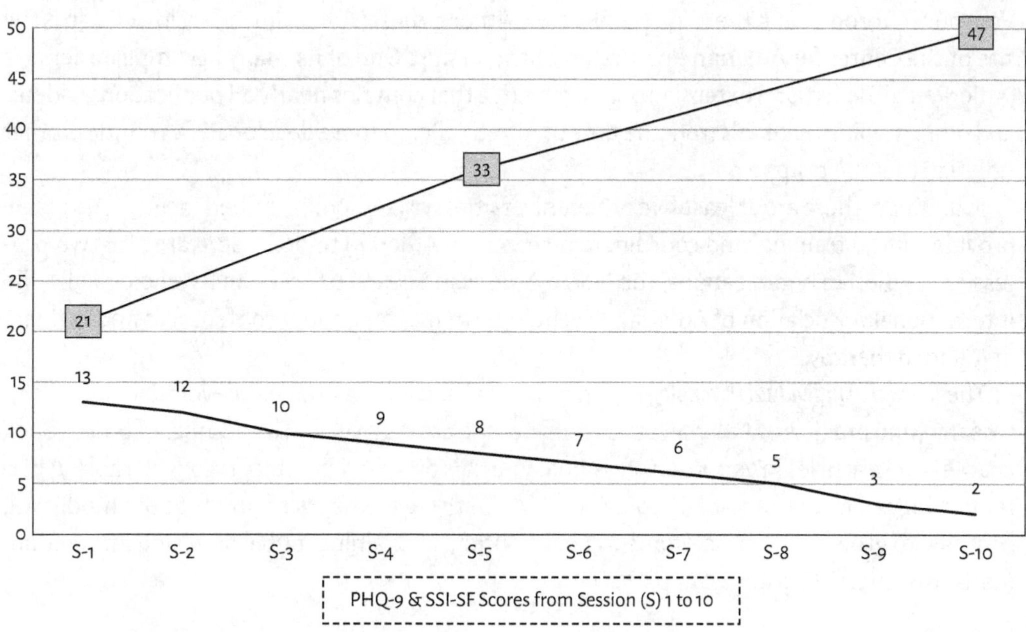

The Future and Challenges of Adlerian Therapy

As previously noted, Adlerian therapy is one of the original psychotherapy approaches, and many of its basic concepts have been incorporated in several current therapeutic approaches (Corey, 2016). It continues to be attractive to graduate students and therapists because it aligns with their own values and goals to make a difference (i.e., social interest). This section discusses the accomplishments and future challenges of Adlerian therapy.

Accomplishments

For practicing therapists as well as trainees, a main attraction of Adlerian therapy has been its flexibility and eclectic approach to treatment. Basically, this means that a therapist can utilize the Adlerian philosophy and assessment approach (i.e., life style assessment) and then plan treatment to incorporate various interventions from the Adlerian approach, as well as any other therapeutic approaches. For many years, this was considered a strength and attractive feature of the Adlerian approach. As we will note in the following section, this attraction has begun to change.

A cursory review of the impacts of this approach over the past several decades is quite telling. Besides its positive influence on the theory and practice of most contemporary approaches, major accomplishments in graduate training, professional publications, and professional organizations reflect how this approach has succeeded in developing and evolving.

Currently, there are many Adlerian therapists around the world who are training the next generation of clinicians and academics in the theory and practice of Adlerian therapy. In North America alone, these include four dedicated Adlerian psychology graduate programs in Chicago, Vancouver, Toronto, and the Minneapolis area. Among these, Adler University in Chicago is the site of the Center for Adlerian Practice and Scholarship. One of its many accomplishments is "AdlerPedia," which is an extensive online resource that contains nearly all publications, videos, and other training materials from the time of Alfred Adler to those developed by countless other Adlerian therapists up to now.

In addition, there are at least five other universities with Adlerian-trained faculty who teach, provide clinical training, and coordinate research on Adlerian topics. There are also two professional Adlerian organizations, the North American Society of Adlerian Psychology and the International Association of Adlerian Psychology, that offer annual conferences and training in Adlerian therapy.

The *Journal of Individual Psychology* is a highly regarded journal that has devoted to the theory, research, and practice of Adlerian psychology for the past 100 years. The number of books, book chapters, and articles in various professional journals on Adlerian topics is considerable. A current listing is available on AdlerPedia (2018). "All of these elements ensure that the model will continue to grow and that Adlerians will have outlets for training, publishing, and interaction" (Carlson & Englar-Carlson, 2017, p. 113).

Challenges

A recent report indicates that while most graduate students preferred Adlerian therapy as a theoretical approach, most said they would practice cognitive behavior therapy instead. The reason? Cognitive behavior therapy is an evidence-based approach and reimbursable, whereas Adlerian therapy is not evidence based and soon may no longer be reimbursable (Glenn, 2015). Students said that the Adlerian approach was much more compatible with their basic beliefs and values, compared to the underlying theory of conventional cognitive behavior therapy. Essentially, these students felt torn between an approach they admired and one that they could be paid for practicing.

The underlying consideration facing both students and practicing therapists is the increasing demand for accountability in providing therapy services. Specifically, reimbursement for professional services by physicians, as well as mental health professionals, is increasing based on documentation that evidence-based treatments were utilized. While a number of contemporary therapy approaches are considered evidence based, Adlerian therapy is not currently considered an evidence-based approach.

Because one of its key intervention components is already a recognized evidence-based approach, Adlerian pattern-focused therapy is more likely than other current Adlerian therapeutic approaches to achieve the status of becoming an evidence-based approach. This status will require the requisite research support, which must include clinical trials.

A related challenge is a needed shift in attitude among some Adlerian therapists. The reality is that many therapists today, including some Adlerian therapists, are wary of embracing evidence-based or documenting treatment outcomes. In fact, "many Adlerians have been much less focused on outcomes and have been satisfied with anecdotal information on the efficacy of the approaches we have used. There is a need for Adlerians to engage in research on the work and the interventions used" (Carlson & Englar-Carlson, 2017, p. 126).

Concluding Note

The purpose of this book was to give readers an up-to-date account of the status of the theory and practice of Adlerian therapy. We accomplished this by reviewing the conventional theory and practice of Adlerian Therapy in the first two chapters. Then, we shifted to a description and illustration of a contemporary view of an Adlerian-informed therapy practice that can meet the needs of students and practicing therapists who are expected to provide and document a more accountable treatment approach. Accordingly, we described Adlerian pattern-focused therapy in chapter 3. We then illustrated its practice in the remaining chapters. We were quite intentional in offering the reader an experiential immersion in the therapy process itself, using extensive clips from the transcription of the entire completed therapy. Finally, we provided an insider's view of the therapy process with extensive commentaries. The interested reader will find the complete transcriptions of all 10 sessions, in their entirety, on the website that accompanies this book.

The purpose of this chapter was to help the reader understand why Jennifer's therapy was so successful. However, it is important to note that not all individuals with moderate levels of depression who receive only psychotherapy without medication will improve as did Jennifer, or do as well as individuals with a mild level of depression. Because of the high level of fit between Adlerian pattern-focused therapy, the therapist's expertise, and Jennifer's involvement and commitment to therapy, she was able to achieve not only remission of her depression (first order change), but also a necessary change in her pattern (second order change).

At this point, the future of Adlerian therapy appears quite optimistic. This, of course, is contingent on one or more Adlerian therapy approaches, such as Adlerian pattern-focused therapy, engaging in clinical trials and achieving evidence-based status.

References

AdlerPedia (2018). Retrieved from: https://www.adlerpedia.org/

Bordin, E. S. (1994). Theory and research on the therapeutic working alliance: New directions. In A. O. Horvath & L. S. Greenberg (Eds.), *The working alliance: Theory, research, and practice* (pp. 13–37). New York, NY: John Wiley & Sons.

Carlson, J., & Englar-Carlson, M. (2017). *Adlerian psychotherapy*. Washington, DC: American Psychological Association.

Castonguary, L., & Hill. C. (Eds.). (2012). *Transformation in psychotherapy: Corrective experiences across cognitive-behavioral, humanistic, and psychodynamics approaches*. Washington DC: American Psychological Association.

Clark, A. (2002). *Early recollections: Theory and practice in counseling and psychotherapy*. New York, NY: Brunner-Routledge.

Corey, G. (2016). *Theory and practice of counseling and psychotherapy* (10th ed.). Belmont, CA: Brooks-Cole.

Fraser, J., & Solovey, A. (2007). *Second-order change in psychotherapy: The golden thread that unifies effective treatments*. Washington DC: American Psychological Association.

Glenn, K. (2015). Can you relate? *Counseling Today, 58*(5), 48–52.

Goldfried, M. (2012). The corrective experiences: A core principle for therapeutic change. In L. Castonguary & C. Hill (Eds.). *Transformation in psychotherapy: Corrective experiences across cognitive-behavioral, humanistic, and psychodynamics approaches* (pp. 13–29). Washington DC: American Psychological Association.

Good, G., & Beitman, B. (2006). *Counseling and psychotherapy essentials: Integrating theories, skills, and practices*. New York, NY: Norton.

Mosak, H., & DiPietro, R. (2006). *Early recollections: Interpretation method and application*. New York, NY: Routledge.

Livesley, W. (2003). *Practical management of personality disorder*. New York, NY: Guilford.

Sperry, L. (2010). *Core competencies in counseling and psychotherapy: Becoming a highly competent and effective therapist*. New York, NY: Routledge.

Sperry, L. & Carlson, J. (2014). *How master therapists work: Effecting change from the first through the last session and beyond*. New York, NY: Routledge.

Sperry, L. & Sperry, J. (2012). *Case conceptualization: Mastering this competency with ease and confidence*. New York, NY: Routledge.

Index

CPSIA information can be obtained
at www.ICGtesting.com
Printed in the USA
LVHW060245100919
630462LV00003B/20/P

9 781516 536948